The Buddha Diet

A Step-by-Step Guide
to Creating a Positive Relationship
With Food and Eating

By Andy Matzner

Disclaimer

.

Enlightenment is: Eat when you are hungry, sleep when you are tired.

(Zen saying)

How to Use This Book

I have packed a lot into *The Buddha Diet*, a program which represents just about everything I know about developing a positive relationship with food. So there is much to absorb! However, it has to be that way because this isn't a quick-fix. Most weight-management books only provide part of the solution. That is why people so often go back to their old habits. In *The Buddha Diet*, I present to you everything you need in order to make powerful, permanent changes in your life on a deep, soul-level. And that will take some serious work. But aren't you worth it? I believe you are!

My advice is for you to skim through the entire book first so that you get a sense of what is involved. This will also give you an understanding of how the chapters are inter-related with each other. Once you've done that, you can go back to the beginning and start working your way through the program at your own pace.

You'll be doing a great deal of introspection and writing as you go through this program, so it will be helpful to choose a journal or notebook that you can dedicate just for *The Buddha Diet*. And perhaps you have a favorite pen or pencil that you enjoy writing with – use that as well.

As with all of the journal exercises you'll encounter in *The Buddha Diet,* the time you spend considering and then writing the answer to each question is directly connected to the progress you can expect to make. That's because this program works **only** if you do the journaling work. But please believe me - it will make all the difference. A satisfying future awaits you...

Table of Contents

Introduction

There are only two mistakes a person can make along the road to truth: not going all the way, and not starting.

the Buddha

Welcome to *The Buddha Diet*!

Before we jump in, I'd like to explain the title of this book.

Why Buddha?

The story of Siddhartha Gautama (aka "the Buddha") and the principles of Buddhism illustrate a way of thinking about life that can help you develop a healthy, healing relationship with food. In developing this program, I was inspired by how the Buddha's spiritual awakening was directly related to breaking a fast. That is, only after the Buddha **stopped depriving** himself of food did he discover the path to **inner peace**. And the system of thought based on the Buddha's teachings, known as "The Middle Way," includes the important ideas of moderation, balance, introspection, self-acceptance, and mindfulness.

Why Diet?

In common usage, diets are eating regimens that people start – and then stop. Let's face it, in spite of all the food programs that are out there, we know that dieting does not work. Plus, diets distort our relationship with food. But I chose to put that word in the title of my book for two reasons. First, it catches people's attention. After all, it's short-hand for "this is a way to manage your weight." And it is important to me to capture people's attention. But now that I have yours, I want to share my other reason for including "diet" in the title: its original meaning.

"Diet" actually comes from the ancient Greek *"diaita"* meaning "way of life." It is also related to the Greek *"diaitasthai,"* which can refer to how a person leads his or her life. I like the original meaning because it's what separates this program from typical diets: a focus on creating a new lifestyle that leads to permanent – not temporary – change that comes from the inside out. For it will be your mental and emotional state that influences how and what you eat. Yet that is the component that most diets ignore!

I believe the most important factor in creating positive change is your **perspective**. That's why I spend the bulk of *The Buddha Diet* teaching you the mental and emotional skills that will support the "what, when and how" of eating. With my program, you'll be set up for success from the beginning!

My goal with *The Buddha Diet* is to help you develop a pleasant, non-combative relationship with food. In the end you'll be making decisions about food based on how much you love and care about your body. It will no longer make sense to you to eat something that you know won't serve your body's best interest. It's as simple as that.

***

What you have before you in this book is everything I have learned as a psychotherapist about how to develop a positive relationship with food and eating.

But what do I mean by "relationship"? A relationship is a connection or association between two things. And when it comes to food, we are literally and figuratively connected to what we choose to put in our mouths.

Multiple times throughout the day we make intellectual, practical, and emotional decisions about what to eat or what to avoid eating. There are some foods we might eat every day, others once in a blue moon, and still others that we deeply desire but refrain from eating (for whatever reason). We might crave and then gobble down a certain food that makes us feel physically sick after we've eaten it. Or we might eat a particular food as a reward because it reminds us of good childhood times. And some food we might not be crazy about, but force ourselves to eat because "the doctor said so."

You can see that we are bound to food in many different ways. But food is bound to us, as well. After all, a good portion of what we consume physically becomes part of our bodies. No relationship could be more intimate.

I would like to believe that (ideally) people choose to be in relationships with one another because each person has the other person's best interests at heart. Each person

● ● ●
3

cares about the other, and wants only the best for their partner. Of course, this doesn't always happen, and it's easy to see that the world is full of dysfunctional relationships.

But consider this: What is the purpose of a relationship? Is it to be draining? Or is it to be energizing? I think answering those questions form a good litmus test for any relationship. Basically, a relationship that drains energy is not healthy! On the other hand, a partnership which is mutually affirming is empowering.

Now think about food, and your connection both with food items and how you eat them. Do you look forward to eating? Does your food give you energy and satisfaction? Or is your relationship with food and eating fraught with guilt, shame, confusion, self-hate and ambivalence?

In *The Buddha Diet*, you will be closely examining, perhaps for the first time, your relationship with food. Doing so is a worthy endeavor, since it is such a vital part of your life. Whether you are deciding what to eat or that you simply won't eat, your connection with food lasts from birth right up until death.

It is my belief that you deserve a positive, healthy, healing relationship with food. Unfortunately, all sorts of things happen to mess that relationship up, from family dynamics, to messages from the media, to feelings of self-worth. But now is the time for you to make that relationship the best it can be: Simple, intuitive, clear. And most importantly, full of love.

The positive changes you'll be experiencing as you go through this program will change your life forever – if you give yourself permission to do what's involved. I do think you'll be very proud of what you have accomplished once you've worked your way to the end of *The Buddha Diet*. Certainly, like anything else worthwhile, it will take commitment, persistence, and patience. Plus the faith that you're doing the right thing for yourself. But just the fact that you're reading these words indicates to me that you are ready to embark on this path.

***

If I had to summarize the overarching principle behind *The Buddha Diet*, I would simply say that it is the power of **self-love**. That is, the key to developing a positive, healthy relationship to food and eating comes from feeling good about yourself, respecting yourself, and treating yourself kindly. Once you learn self-love, your connection with food will naturally change. By accepting yourself without judgment (through unconditional self-love), you will effortlessly gravitate towards healthy, satisfying food choices. With self-love, eating ceases to be a chore or something you have to force yourself to do. After all, motivation powered by unhappiness and resentment toward your own body is bound to fail. This is why the traditional diets so many people follow are so problematic.

But people often have a difficult time showing themselves self-love. I have experienced this as a psychotherapist, working with clients who:

- o Engaged in self-sabotage
- o Acted against their own self-interest
- o Could not imagine treating themselves with kindness and compassion

- Persisted in behavior that they knew was harmful
- Believed they didn't deserve anything nice to happen to them

So what prevents a person from being kind to him or herself? I have found that there are three major barriers that keep a person from treating him or herself with compassion and kindness. These are:

- Maladaptive belief systems
- Negative self-talk
- The inner critic

In *The Buddha Diet* I will teach you how to address and neutralize these obstacles. In addition, I will share other important skills that will enable you to develop a healthy relationship with yourself (and food). These include the ability to:

- Be fully present in one's life
- Connect with core values
- Manage difficult feelings in a positive manner

And since so many people use food as a way to cope with painful feelings, I will share strategies for dealing with emotional eating.

You'll also spend a lot of time in *The Buddha Diet* learning how to develop love, understanding, and compassion for yourself. Doing so will lead to your ability to:

- Pay attention to yourself
- Acknowledge your inherent value

o   Accept yourself as you are (and as you have been in the past)
o   Cultivate a sense of gratitude
o   Nurture yourself without feeling guilty

***

Eight skills form the core of *The Buddha Diet*. They are the keys to developing a positive relationship with yourself and how you eat.

Skill #1: Mindfulness

I begin with mindfulness (and its various aspects of concentration, attention, non-judgment and acceptance) because it greatly influences what you choose to eat, the manner in which you eat it, and how much you consume. Approaching food and eating with mindfulness will have an immense impact on your relationship with food and eating. The ability to be mindful will also make mastering the other skills much easier.

Skill #2: Accessing Authentic Values

By creating a connection with your deepest values, you will be able to lay the foundation for success in future change, especially with food and eating. Being clear and comfortable about who you are and what you stand for creates the motivation and commitment necessary for positive change. Most importantly, by becoming aligned with your true values, you will develop the ability to make ***the*** right choice when faced with a decision about ***anything***, including food and eating.

Skill #3: Cultivating Self-Compassion

In order to create lasting, positive change you must first fully accept yourself as you are. This means that you also have to be willing to accept *where* you are in life. Self-rejection does not support growth. If you like yourself, you will treat yourself kindly. Accordingly, if you care about your body, you will naturally choose the foods that are right for it.

Skill #4: Overcoming Maladaptive Underlying Beliefs

One of the most important questions you can ask yourself is, "Where did my basic assumptions and ideas about myself and the world around me come from?" It is your belief system that will prevent you from creating and maintaining a positive, healthy relationship with food and eating. In this section of the book, I explain how to carefully examine the values, assumptions, ideals and ideologies which influence (and constrain) the way you think, feel and act. Then I present the tools that will allow you to develop a new belief system which conceptualizes food and eating in a positive, empowering way.

Skill #5: Neutralizing Negative Self-Talk

Another road-block to positive change is negative thinking and self-talk, which generally flows from your negative belief system. When you talk to yourself, you may tell yourself things that make you feel badly about yourself or your life. Your inner monologue may sound rational and accurate, but in reality these messages only serve to keep you feeling bad about yourself by provoking feelings such as anxiety, depression, and low-self-esteem. Because you generally listen to – and take seriously – these internal voices, they have the power to influence your perception of reality. I will give you the tools to challenge them.

Skill #6: Disarming "The Inner Critic"

In this chapter I specifically examine "the inner critic," that destructive voice in your head that offers judgmental commentary, usually on a regular basis. The inner critic often stops you from making positive changes in your life. It often can prevent you from making decisions that are in your best interests, particularly when it comes to food and eating. I teach you to understand who your critic is, how to get in touch with what your critic is telling you, and then how to decide what to actually do about it.

Skill #7: Managing Emotional Eating

People use food to manipulate their emotions for a variety of reasons. In this chapter I examine those reasons, and present strategies for overcoming emotional eating. You will learn how to identify and manage triggers that lead to emotional eating, as well as how to deal with food cravings triggered by difficult emotions.

Skill #8: Dealing with Emotions

If emotional eating is no longer an option, then what kinds of strategies will you use when difficult emotions do arise? In this chapter you will discover how to manage your emotions in a healthy way.

By learning each of these skills and incorporating them into your life, you will be able to create the relationship with food that you truly desire, one that is free of drama, discipline, and regret. An added benefit is that mastering these skills will improve the quality of your life in general.

While I present each of the skills to you in a linear fashion, beginning with mindfulness and ending with managing emotions, I would prefer that you not think of them as a rigid sequence of single steps. Instead, I'd like you to view these eight skills as interdependent principles that act in a supportive relationship with each other. Consider them as interweaving threads that create a unified whole. As a group, they are much more powerful than their individual components. By acting synergistically, they will give you the ability to have a healthy relationship with food and eating.

***

Now it is time to truly begin! We will start with some journaling. Please find a safe, comfortable space, and make sure you won't be disturbed, as you'll need to give yourself enough time to answer the questions I have for you.

I've included these specific questions because it is important for you to be honest with yourself as you begin this beautiful – but challenging – journey to achieving peace with food. They set the tone for all that will follow. Remember: There are no right nor wrong answers. The key is to relax and simply write down what comes to your mind. Don't over-think things; just follow your intuition, and allow yourself to express what emerges into your consciousness.

As you think about *The Buddha Diet* and what it might mean for you...

- What excites you about this program?
- What concerns do you have?
- How will your daily schedule reflect your commitment to this book?
- What will you have to stop doing in order to have the energy to engage in this program?
- What are the implications for you if you decide to put this off?

And:

- How does it feel to be in uncharted territory?
- When presented with something new, do you find yourself being open or skeptical?
- How do you feel about taking risks? How does it feel to take a risk?
- What message can you tell yourself that will allow you to "feel the fear and do it anyway"?
- What can you do to easily remind yourself of this message while you are working your way through *The Buddha Diet*?
- What kind of support can you set up for yourself as you do this work?

***

- Is unconditional permission to eat scary? Why?
- Do you believe that you can have a healthy relationship with food?
    - Do you have to give yourself permission first in order to do that?
    - If so, exactly how would you do that?
- How might your current relationship with food and eating be a metaphor for your life in general?

- In order to have a new, positive relationship with food:

    - What would you have to let go of?
    - What would you have to accept?
    - What would you have to be willing to do?

Chapter 1

What the Buddha Discovered (About Dieting)

Peace comes from within. Do not seek it without.

the Buddha

I have found that when it comes to weight management and healthy eating, most people decide to follow some kind of restrictive diet. The diet's success typically depends on how "strong" a person's willpower is. Unfortunately, when I think of willpower, the following comes to mind:

- Doing something I don't *really* want to do
- Doing something I *should* do, because it's the *right thing* to do
- Fighting against another part of me that wants to do something else
- Forcing myself to do something that doesn't come naturally
- Expending a great amount of effort to do something that doesn't come easily

As you can see, when a person's relationship with food is dependent on willpower, it becomes bound up with struggle and negativity. After all, we can force ourselves to do something we don't really want to do only for so long. For this reason, a relationship with food based on deprivation, discipline and self-regulation will almost always fail. So is there another way to have a relationship with food? I believe there is, and I would like to share it with you.

The Story of the Buddha

During the mid-6th century BCE, Siddhartha Gautama, who later became known as the Buddha, was born in modern-day Nepal near the Indian border. As the child of a wealthy royal family, Siddhartha was raised in luxury. Despite his father's attempts to shield him from the realities of life, one day the curious Siddhartha ventured out beyond the castle walls and encountered three aspects of life that no one can escape: old age, sickness and death. Siddhartha also encountered a holy man who, by choice, was living a life of austerity. Although deprived of life's comforts, the ascetic appeared at peace. This experience greatly moved Siddhartha, and he decided to renounce his comfortable lifestyle in order to go out into the world and search for the "truth" about why suffering existed – and what to do about it.

Initially, Siddhartha believed that his physical body was an impure barrier between him and enlightenment. Therefore, he spent time practicing extreme forms of self-denial, believing that deprivation would lead to liberation from the suffering of old age, death and rebirth. In particular, Siddhartha greatly limited what he ate, consuming only a grain of rice and one sesame seed each day. It wasn't long before he became so thin that he could touch his spine by pressing on his stomach. After six years of this self-punishment, Siddhartha discovered that he no longer had the strength to meditate. His spirit was dull. He was physically and mentally exhausted. And most distressing, he found that in spite of all his efforts he was no closer to his goals than when he had started.

Realizing that self-punishment was a dead-end (literally, as he was close to death), Siddhartha reconsidered his strategy. While he knew that his former life of wealth and self-indulgence would have led him far away from "the truth," Siddhartha now believed as well that no one could achieve a higher state of being through deprivation.

It was at this very moment that Siddhartha happened to hear a lute player strumming his instrument. Noticing how the different tensions of each string created various qualities of sound, Siddhartha suddenly had an epiphany: if a string is too loose its sound is dull and muddy. Too tight, it squeaks – and often breaks. Instead, the player can produce a beautiful tone only when the lute is tuned precisely – with its strings neither too taut nor too slack.

Based on this observation, Siddhartha concluded that the body had to be nourished and physically fit. In addition, the body was an equal partner with the mind – it was wrong to privilege one over the other. Siddhartha decided that the proper way to create harmony between the body and mind would be through moderation and balance: The Middle Path.

At this point a village girl, seeing his emaciated state, offered Siddhartha a meal of milk porridge, which he accepted. Having regained his strength and considering what to do next, Siddhartha sat under a tree and found himself reminded of a childhood experience when had been at the Ploughing Festival one beautiful spring day. Left alone while his retinue enjoyed the festivities, the young Siddhartha, under the cool shade of a rose-apple tree, had begun focusing on his breath. In doing so, he discovered that he could access a deep state of meditative peace. This memory, long forgotten until now, inspired Siddhartha. He realized that meditation would lead him to the knowledge he sought. Siddhartha then vowed to himself that he would remain seated under the tree until he achieved enlightenment – which, after forty-nine days, he did. And henceforth Siddhartha was known as "Buddha," "the awakened one".

Self-punishment and deprivation require discipline and strength. But Siddhartha recognized that such effort, while devoted, is misdirected, since the body is not the enemy. Instead, he learned that the path to understanding is a balanced approach to life that honors body, soul, and mind. It is significant that Siddhartha finally reached understanding about the human condition after he began to nurture his body by eating normally again. It is this aspect of the Buddha's life – his decision to show himself compassion and embrace moderation – that is the key to *The Buddha Diet.*

What is especially striking to me is how Siddhartha realized that his deprivation was doing him no good. *For the more he tried, the further away he moved from his goal...*

Interestingly, what the Buddha experienced 2500 years ago is known today as *The Law of Reversed Effort*. According to this principle, the harder you try to do something that otherwise comes naturally to the body, the less likely you will be successful at it. For example, have you ever tried to force yourself to fall asleep? Or, having forgotten somebody's name, have you ever attempted to force yourself to remember it? What about riding a bicycle? Have you ever noticed the difference between paying attention to how you were balancing on two wheels versus just pushing off and going? These examples show how the more pressure you put on controlling your subconscious, the more difficult it will be to achieve. And nowhere else is this more evident than with eating.

Your body *naturally* knows when it is hungry and when it is satisfied. But when you try to manipulate those physiological aspects – eating when you're not hungry, denying yourself food when you *are* hungry – your body rebels. It just doesn't feel right. The same goes for your brain – it goes into alarm mode because it knows things aren't the way they should be. And so it releases chemicals that cause you to feel stressed, anxious, depressed, agitated....

Thus, what the Buddha discovered most of us know only too well – diets are problematic because they cause people to feel deprived, triggering emotional and behavioral rebellion. Diets also initiate a person's starvation mode, which causes hormonal imbalances; when the body perceives the danger of starvation, it hoards calories and fat for safety. Finally, diets don't work because they focus on the wrong target (food), instead of the underlying emotions that cause people to create an unhealthy relationship with food in the first place.

Like trying to squeeze a fistful of water, the Buddha's decision to conquer his body's true needs led only to frustration. Instead, it was self-compassion that led the Buddha to a relationship with food that was satisfying.

In the end, what the Buddha learned was that the less effort he expended, the better he felt. By giving up his desire to control a natural process, the easier it became to truly nurture and honor his body. But this idea is radical in the modern world of dieting, which is centered on unrealistic images of beauty, and focused on controlling and measuring the intake of food to meet those standards.

The Four Noble Truths

Based on his experiences, the Buddha developed a philosophy of life known as "The four noble truths." These ideas, which I list below, explain how and why people experience distress in their lives, plus the way to find relief.

1. **Life is painful.** No matter how much we want to permanently achieve happiness, the truth is that just by being alive, we will encounter pain and suffering; we simply cannot avoid it.

2. **The origin of our suffering is attachment.** We want to hold onto our happiness and the objects in our lives that give us pleasure. We want to remain young and healthy. We also want the people we care about to be healthy and remain alive. On the

other hand, we want to avoid things and situations that are painful. The Buddha believed that these desires lead to unhappiness because nothing ever stays the same; life is always in a state of change. Difficulty occurs when we want the good things to stay the same forever and the bad things to hurry up and be over with. We want to always feel healthy. We don't want to get sick or old. And we certainly don't want to die. In reality, however, everything is always in a state of flux. Nothing in this world is permanent. Wishing things were different than they are always leads to frustration and disappointment.

The Buddha also emphasized that our cravings for things cause us deep pain. This is because the dissatisfaction that fuels our desires doesn't go away when we finally get what we were chasing. For once we *do* possess something we wanted, we then end up clinging to it, wishing it would remain unchanged forever. This only leads to suffering, since it is the nature of everything in this world to change. In spite of all our efforts, some form of loss is always inevitable.

3. **However, it *is* possible to escape suffering.** This is done by relinquishing our cravings, and refusing to cling to what we already possess. We can experience contentment when we acknowledge and make peace with the idea that life is always in a state of change, and that nothing lasts forever.

4. **The blueprint for ending suffering is found by following "the eightfold path:"** *Right view; right intention; right speech; right action; right livelihood; right effort; right mindfulness; right concentration.* These are a series of practical methods that lead to a new way of living life. By being deliberate with our actions, intentional with our words, and mindful of our thoughts and feelings, it is possible to live a life free from frustration and disappointment.

In crafting this book, I was inspired by the four noble truths and the eightfold path. The story of the Buddha and his philosophy of life contain everything you need to gain the insight and ability to leave dieting behind forever.

After all, you know that using dieting, discipline and restrictive eating to manage your weight only leads to frustration and disappointment. These methods do not work because they attempt to control the natural processes of hunger and satiety. Instead of listening to the individual reality of your body, diets emphasize eating a particular way so that you can meet a particular standard (which may not be natural for your body). In addition, our society's powerful message is that you will not be happy or attractive to others until you look a certain way and weigh a specific amount. All this fruitless chasing after impossible ideals – no wonder dieting saps energy and produces misery!

There is a way to avoid this misery, however. It is by examining your motives for managing your weight and exploring your current relationship with food. This understanding, along with your desire to approach food and eating with intention, deliberation, and mindfulness, will lead to a more satisfying life in general. In particular, your decision to pay attention to how you treat yourself and the world around you will lead to the development of the self-compassion that will allow you to change your relationship with food and eating forever.

***

Embracing what the Buddha discovered means making some significant changes in the way you think about the purpose and role of food in your life. But how will you make sure the changes you make actually stick? As you know, many people set goals and jump into new ways of thinking and behaving – only to give up and go back to their old ways. So what if we explored how the process of "change" actually works? I believe that a clear understanding of this process will set the stage for your success with this program. This is because the popular belief that people can only change by using their **willpower** is wrong and only leads to frustration. Instead, you will see that true, lasting change comes about when you are able to treat yourself with kindness and compassion. Just remember what the Buddha learned!

Chapter 2

How to Change (Or Not)

We cannot solve our problems with the same thinking we used when we created them.

Albert Einstein

To heal a suffering one must experience it to the full.

Marcel Proust

We cannot change anything until we accept it. Condemnation does not liberate, it oppresses.

Carl Jung

True mastery can be gained by letting things go their own way. It can't be gained by interfering.

Lao Tzu

Whether it is a New Year's resolution or the latest diet, forcing ourselves to change because we "should" typically proves frustrating and disappointing. As I discussed in the last chapter, changing because you *have to* rarely works long-term because this type of change is dependent on **willpower**. In effect, you are at war with yourself. There is a part of you who wants to change, while at the same time there is another part of you that wants to stay the same. This forces a person to expend a great deal of effort in creating and maintaining change. Because that tension is always present, true change is impossible.

So here is something to consider: What if, instead of trying to force yourself to make a change, you first took some time to settle into your current self? That is, what if you stopped trying to be something you are not, and made a decision to simply accept yourself as you are, today? I believe that by doing so, the energy that you've been expending in the battle between trying to change and resisting change suddenly becomes available for other, more productive, uses.

Of course you might naturally ask, How does "giving up and settling in" actually create change? I have found that **when the time is ripe**, change will happen **naturally**, without being forced. The essential ingredient is your intention. Your intention to be open. Your intention to follow your intuition. Your intention to let this process unfold in its own time, without forcing it.

My belief is that a heightened awareness of our current state is what actually allows change to occur. That is, in order to step into our future, we must **first** be fully engaged in the reality of our present life. This means that change must begin from our life as it is, not from how we would like it to be. Therefore, our first task, when it comes to change, is to consider and then accept the reality of our lives, both past and present. We also have to make peace with and take responsibility for our past and present choices. In doing so, we can be fully aware of our current position in life.

> *Change can occur when [a person] abandons, at least for the moment, what he would like to become and attempts to be what he is. The premise is that one must stand in one place in order to have firm footing to move and that it is difficult or impossible to move without that footing.* (Arnold Beisser)

As we explore who we think we are, and then discover who we really are, we reach the deepest core of our being. This is why I have filled *The Buddha Diet* with introspective journaling exercises. You will encounter questions that will make you think deeply and honestly about your life, questions that will compel you to take inventory. I want to challenge the values and assumptions that have guided you up to this point, and have caused you to have the current relationship you have with food and eating – a relationship I assume you would like to change.

> *Questioning is a basic tool for rebellion. It breaks open the stagnant hardened shells of the present, revealing ambiguity and opening up fresh options to be explored...Questioning can change your entire life. It can uncover hidden power and stifled dreams inside of you...things you may have denied for many years.* (Fran Peavey)

The journaling work you do during this program will allow you to discover – and discard – those parts of yourself (ideas, beliefs, personas) that no longer serve your best interests. As you consider your life, you will understand that you have unlived potential just waiting to be realized. Think of the resulting emptiness as fertile soil, in which space has been created for your true self to emerge and grow.

But facing our reality is typically not easy. Because the process makes us feel vulnerable, we generally avoid it. However, the process of going back so that we can go forward, while painful, is essential to our lives if we truly desire peace.

So this is the paradox of change. First, we must release our conscious desire to change. Next, we must fully embrace our present selves – who and where we are now. With that awareness, we can face our wounds and fears. We can dissolve what is blocking us and learn to live in the here and now. Then – and only then – by recognizing and dealing with unfinished business from the past and in the present, can we begin to consider, and perhaps even follow, other potential paths that resonate more deeply within us.

It is only when our delusions have been stripped away and we have our feet firmly planted in the reality of our lives, that we can gradually begin to move forward again, embracing our possibilities and our futures because we are no longer encumbered by the baggage of our past. With the resulting awareness and insight, the change that had been impossible for us will emerge spontaneously and authentically. That is, we will **intuitively** make the decisions that are right for us. No effort or force required!

The most important thing to remember is that when you are ready to change, you will. Not sooner and not later. So it is fine if you don't yet feel compelled to make changes in your life. Don't force yourself to be somewhere that you don't *yet* belong. After all, change can be scary because it is unpredictable. And if the perceived pain of change outweighs the pain of staying the same, you might spend a long time simply thinking about changing without taking any concrete action. Which is OK, if that is where you are.

A way to make sense of this is to consider your location on the **Stages of Change** model (developed by psychologist James Prochaska). These five stages describe the process a person passes through on their way to creating and maintaining change. People move from stage to stage organically, in their own time, when they are ready. A person can't be forced to move from one stage to another, either by guilt or by other people. The most important thing is to accept our current stage, and recognize that we will move to the next stage when the time is right.

- The **precontemplation** stage is when you are unaware there is a problem, and therefore you have no desire to change.
- You move into the **contemplation** stage when you begin to think that there *might* be a something in your life that needs to change. During this time, you'll be on the fence about whether or not to commit to changing.
- In the **preparation** stage you've made up your mind to take action. You begin to take concrete steps to prepare to make a change, gearing up for doing the actual work related to accomplishing your goal.

- During the **Action** Stage you are actively engaged in new behaviors related to achieving your goal. You are consciously working on creating concrete changes in your life and are fully committed to changing.
- In the **maintenance** stage, you have accomplished your goal and have been living a lifestyle that is congruent with your values for an extended amount of time.
- **Relapse** refers to occasions when you slip back into old, unhealthy habits. When this occurs, it is time to revisit your core values and learn from the experience of relapsing so that it doesn't happen again.

The journaling exercises in *The Buddha Diet* are vital because they are designed to create the opportunity for cultivating self-knowledge. Through introspection and self-inquiry, you can begin to create the conditions for change to occur naturally. This is because *the right questions* are the most effective tools for moving a person from the precontemplation stage to the preparation stage.

When you learn about yourself, become comfortable with who you are, and unconditionally accept yourself (for better or worse), then – paradoxically – you will begin to move in a direction that is right for you.

So before you focus on making concrete changes in your life regarding food and eating, I would like you to simply spend some time thinking about yourself and your life (past and present). There will be times when I will also ask you to use your imagination to think about the future. I believe that doing all of this will lead you to exactly where you need to go. In fact, that is what the majority of *The Buddha Diet* consists of – introspection that is meant to lead to self-acceptance. The effort you expend now learning more about yourself will dramatically change the relationship you currently have with food and eating.

Remember to find a safe, comfortable space where you can be alone and undisturbed as you write. Your journal time is sacred and the right atmosphere is vital. Take your time and do what is necessary to center yourself. Perhaps light some incense or candles. Then, with your journal before you, take some deep, cleansing breaths in order to clear your mind. Your goal is to access your intuitive voice. This is the part of you that resides deep in your soul and is just waiting to express itself to you. It is you being honest with yourself, simply because it is time.

To begin:

- Divide up a piece of paper into four quarters. At the top of each put the following headings:
    - Advantages of keeping your current food/eating habits
    - Disadvantages of keeping your current food/eating habits
    - Advantages of changing your current relationship with food
    - Disadvantages of changing your current relationship with food

Once you have filled in each of the four quadrants, take some time to study what you have written. What do your lists tell you about your current way of eating? Do they give you a new perspective about your food habits? Does what you have written affect your commitment to *The Buddha Diet*? If so, how?

Journal Questions

- What do you think it might cost you in the future if you do not make a change in your eating habits?
- What costs have you already experienced in the past due to food/eating issues?

- If you make a change, what positive things do you think might occur in the future?
- If you make a change, what negative things might occur?

- How will your change in eating habits positively affect the people around you?
- How will your change negatively affect people in your life?

- Imagine that it is many years from now and you are nearing the end of your life. Pretend that you had decided NOT to make a change in your eating habits.
    - What were the consequences of your decision on your health?
    - On your relationships?
    - On your sense of well-being?
    - On your body?

- It is five years from now and you have made a decision to go in a particular direction in regards to how you eat. Close your eyes and use your imagination...how does that future feel and look to you? What do you notice? What's going on around you? Are you glad you made the decisions you did? Are you satisfied with the changes that have occurred in your life? Why?

Now let's examine what might be holding you back from making changes that are in your best interest. Please respond to the following in your journal:

- Fill in the rest of this sentence:
  - The problem with having a healthy relationship with food is:

- In order to have a healthy relationship with food, what would you have to do? What would you have to give up? At this point, why do you think you might be willing to pay that price?

- Why is it important for you to have a healthy relationship with food?

- If weight loss is an issue for you, please answer the following:
  - The problem with losing weight is:
  - In order to lose weight, I would have to:
  - It is important for me to lose weight because:

Once you have finished the journal questions, take some time to check in with yourself. How do you feel about moving forward with this program? What about your motivation level? Where are you on the "stages of change"? Has developing a healthy relationship with food become even more important to you? Why or why not?

Chapter 3

Food and Eating:

Practical Considerations

The "Why" of Eating

Ostensibly, we eat when we are hungry in order to provide energy and nutrients for our body. So what are some reasons we might eat when we are not hungry? Consider the following list:

- Not listening to what our stomach is telling us (for example, we might keep eating even though we already feel full)
- Confusing hunger with being thirsty
- Being unable to achieve a feeling of satisfaction with what is being eaten, and so continuing to eat
- Having a meal just because the clock says it's time to eat
- Having a sense of obligation to finish what is on the plate
- Feeling any one of a number of emotions that bring on the urge to eat
- Feeling that the food tastes too good not to eat
- Feeling bored
- Feeling tired

- Being worried about offending someone if the food isn't eaten
- Being influenced by advertising and marketing
- Using food as a reward
- Eating in order to celebrate
- Using food as self-punishment
- Eating out of habit
- Eating food because it is there
- Being attracted to a certain food because it brings back memories (smell, taste, texture)
- Using food to avoid pain
- Using food in order to self-soothe

Journal Questions

What are some of the reasons you eat when you are not hungry?

What are the costs to you of eating when you are not hungry?

Is it possible to eat when you are not hungry – and still enjoy doing so without feeling guilty afterwards?

Ideally, for you personally, what *should* be the purpose of eating?

The "When" of eating

Nature operates on the rhythmic principle of ebb and flow, contraction and expansion. Each year has its seasonal cycle. Each day has its time of dark and light. Each moment you are breathing in and then breathing out. Everything in the universe is in rhythmic motion, right down to the pulsations of energy particles at the deepest quantum level.

So it is with hunger and fullness. Taking food into your body (and refraining from doing so) is part of an eternal cycle you will experience as long as you are alive. As you move throughout your morning, day, and evening, your body will naturally give you cues as to how hungry and how satisfied it is. The issue is, first, how aware are you of those messages? And second, how willing are you to respect them?

Simply stated, peace with food means listening to your body and eating when you are hungry. Peace with food means finishing your meal when you are no longer hungry, but instead feel satisfied (**before** you feel the fullness in your belly). Peace with food means honoring the role of food in your life as a gift of nurturance, and not using food as a way to get other needs met.

So – How will you know when you are truly hungry? How will you know when you are really satisfied and can stop eating? And what if you feel lost because you are unfamiliar with these sensations?

It is time to re-learn those natural feelings of hunger and satisfaction. This can be done by paying close attention to what you are experiencing, physically and mentally. It is vital that you listen to the intuitive wisdom of your body, as it knows exactly when it needs food and when it has had enough. Everything you will learn in *The Buddha Diet* is designed to give you the ability to recognize when your emotional and mental states are interfering with your true hunger and fullness cues. But before we get to the psychological strategies, it is first important for you to become familiar with your own sense of hunger and fullness.

Take a moment to study the following spectrum. It runs from starving to feeling uncomfortably stuffed. "The Hunger Scale" is a tool will give you an easy, convenient way to check in with yourself as you begin to pay attention to your body's need for food. I'll talk more about how to use The Hunger Scale later in this chapter. For now, just familiarize yourself with it.

The Hunger Scale

1. Starving

You are physically ill, feeling light-headed and exhausted, with almost no energy.

2. Ravenous

You are irritable and unable to concentrate; your stomach is empty and you crave food.

3. Very Hungry

You hear your stomach rumbling and gurgling.

4. Hungry

You notice that your energy level is low; the idea of eating food is attractive to you.

5. Slightly hungry

You are beginning to feel hunger pangs; you are not yet compelled to eat but are thinking about your next meal.

6. Satisfied

You feel perfectly comfortable and energized, and notice that you cannot feel the food in your stomach; you feel neither hungry nor full.

7. Mildly full

You notice a slight sense of pressure in your stomach.

8. Full

You can feel the heaviness of the food you've just eaten in your stomach; you need to loosen your clothes

9. Uncomfortably full

You are bloated and tired. You feel heavy and need to lie down.

10. Stuffed

You are miserable, feeling sick to your stomach. The thought of food disgusts you.

From now on, when you are making a choice about what to eat for a meal or a snack, I would like you to take a deep breath and then ask yourself:

- Where am I on the hunger scale? Am I *physically* hungry?
- Do I want to eat in order to change the way I am feeling?
- Do I actually want what I am gravitating towards?
- Will I feel deprived if I don't eat it?
- Will my choice be satisfying?
- How does my choice fit into my chosen way of eating?
- Is this food choice worthy of going into my body?
- Does my choice taste good?
- Will I feel guilty if I eat this?

(These questions might be difficult to answer now, but once you learn the skill of mindfulness in the next chapter, you will be able to get a more accurate sense of your hunger and fullness.)

Before you eat something, one of the most important things you can do is close your eyes and project yourself into the future. You've been down this path thousands of times already – intuitively you already know how eating certain foods (and particular quantities of those foods) will make you feel afterwards. But now I would like you to deliberately consider the consequences of your action in order to see if it will really be worth it. So simply give yourself the following message:

"Let me imagine how I will feel after I have eaten what I am about to eat...Am I OK with the consequences?"

Finally, if you are aware that you are truly hungry for food, here are two good questions to ask yourself that your intuition will always be able to answer:

- Is the food that I have chosen nourishing for my body? What nutrients does it actually provide for me?
- If eating this particular food isn't in my best interest, then what foods would best nourish me at this time?

As you begin to regularly tune into your body during the day, and as you eat your meals, you will soon become quite familiar with The Hunger Scale. With the passage of time and experience, and as you work your way through this book, you will learn to quickly recognize where you are on the scale, and then how to respond.

The "How" of Eating

Our personal histories often influence how we approach food and eating. Understanding your past will allow you to see how you developed your current relationship with food. It is vital to explore these connections so that you can recognize and then break old patterns that no longer serve you.

Please complete the following in your journal:

- My favorite childhood foods were:
- Typical family breakfasts took place in the following location:
- Typical family dinners took place in the following location:
- True or False: I looked forward to family meals.
    - Please explain why or why not.
- A typical family meal felt:
- The things that we often talked about during meals were:
- The rules in my family surrounding eating and meals consisted of:
- Growing up, the main lessons I learned about making and eating food were:
- My two most positive childhood memories regarding food are:
- My two most disturbing childhood memories regarding food are:
- Five words that characterize my mother's relationship with food and cooking are:
- Five words that characterize my father's relationship with food and cooking are:

- Some things I learned as a child or teenager about food and eating that are still part of my life today are:
- Some messages about my body that I learned from my family were:
- I first began to manipulate my eating habits and hunger when:
    - The thing that happened that led me to that change was:
- Some examples of the different ways I have manipulated my eating habits and hunger are:
    - The consequences of doing so have been:

Now please answer the following questions about your current eating situation:

- How do you plan your weekly menu? Are your meals well thought-out in advance?
- Do you eat at the same times each day?
- What is breakfast like for you? Is it rushed? Leisurely?
- How are your dinners structured? Do you look forward to them?
- What would you have to give up in order to spend more time and energy planning, preparing, and eating your meals? Why might it be worth it?
- How willing are you to consider some new ways to plan, prepare and eat your meals? If you are not totally willing, what would have to change for you to increase your motivation?

The next sections in this chapter will provide a framework of each of your meals. Knowing when (and how) to start and stop eating will be essential to the development of your new, positive relationship with food.

Beginning your meal

Consider the rhythm of your life. We all need consistent pacing in our lives, especially with meal times. This is because you can't properly digest food if you are stressed, rushing or distracted. The physiological consequences of stress greatly influence the amount of time food stays in your stomach, as well as how you physically feel it in there. So please consider giving yourself more time to eat. See if you can create an inviting, pleasant environment in which you would enjoy spending time. It is especially important to eat sitting down, using correct posture and not slouching, as that also affects the digestive process.

Of course, you have decided to eat in the first place because you are truly hungry for some food. That is why **The Hunger Scale** is so important. As babies and young children, we are naturally in tune with what our bodies need. But as we grow older we lose the ability to accurately gauge that sense of physical hunger. Instead, we find ourselves eating for all sorts of other reasons (as detailed in the first part of this chapter). Therefore, one of your major goals is to begin to reacquaint yourself with that feeling of true physical hunger. This means taking the time to notice the sensations you feel *below* your neck.
Pay attention to your stomach and your energy level. Physical hunger does not equal the feeling of craving something to eat. Rather, it comes on gradually, without a sense of compulsion. Typically people begin to feel hungry

3-5 hours after their last meal. This means that you will feel the desire to eat in your stomach, not in your heart.

Of course, you don't want to wait until you reach the "starving" or "ravenous" zones on The Hunger Scale, since those often lead to binge eating. For some people getting too physically hungry can lead to irritability, fatigue, headaches, an inability to concentrate, or even dizziness. In addition, feeling your stomach growling and rumbling is also a sign that you have waited too long to eat. Monitoring your physical hunger so that you do not reach those levels of physical discomfort is a vital skill that you must learn. The key is noticing the message your stomach is telling you, and then acting on it instead of ignoring it. As I mentioned above, learning the skill of mindfulness in the next chapter will allow you to be able to differentiate between physical and emotional hunger.

During your meal

Now let's imagine that you have decided that you are physically hungry. Think about what you might experience if you were able to slow yourself down, choosing your food with deliberation and preparing it with care. What if you took some time to appreciate your food's color, texture, and aroma? As you chewed your food thoroughly and attentively, you might discover that as its texture changes with each chew, so does its flavor. At the same time, it is helpful to be conscious of how you are breathing while you eat. A regular, measured flow of oxygen in and carbon dioxide out helps your digestive system do its job properly and with ease. Distracted eating actually leads to less nutrient absorption. Also, typically the more distracted a person is, the more he or she will consume. What about you? Do you tend to watch television or read during your meal? Do you find that when you eat you are disconnected from your food, and are just going through the motions?

Please notice what it feels like to pay attention to what you are eating. See if you can give yourself permission to savor your food. It is helpful if you put down your fork or spoon in-between bites, picking it up again once you've completely chewed your current mouthful of food. Doing so will also aid you in determining when to stop eating (more about that shortly).

After each bite, you can ask yourself:

- How does it feel to eat this food?
- How is this food affecting me?
- Is there a connection between what I just ate and how I feel now?
- What am I noticing that changes with each bite of food?

Finishing your meal

One of the most important things you can do is to stop eating before you feel full. This will take courage and a strong belief in yourself because it will likely be a new – and unfamiliar – way of eating for you. The key is to understand that there will be a point during your meal when you will feel neither hungry nor full. Your goal is to notice when you have more energy than you did when you first sat down to eat. In order to locate that point, simply slow down and pay attention to your energy level as you eat; notice how your stomach feels during your meal. Ideally, you should stop eating **before** you feel anything in your stomach. Unfortunately, by the time you feel the food settling into your stomach, it is too late. Instead, you should be feeling that what you just ate has provided you with a sense of well-being and comfort. Therefore, the point at which you should stop eating is when you are no longer hungry but energized instead. Be sure to avoid being guided by your head (that is, expectations, judgments, thoughts). Instead, let the feelings in your body tell you exactly how much to eat and when to stop.

An easy way to check in with yourself after you have been eating awhile is to ask the following questions:

- "How am I feeling?"
- "How is my energy level?"
- "Am I noticing my stomach?"
- "Am I beginning to feel heaviness in my stomach?"

If you follow this method, you will know **exactly** when to end your meal. It might take some time to learn how to eat this way because it is unfamiliar right now, but once you do you'll never have to weigh food or count calories again!

"The clean plate club"

In the beginning, as you practice this new way of eating, you will discover that it will be difficult to judge how much food to serve yourself. Odds are you will be eating less than you are used to, but you'll still be giving yourself the same portions as before. This means there will be times when you will have to leave some food over on your plate. So despite everything your parents told you about starving children in third world countries, you will have to learn how to be comfortable not finishing what is in front of you. My thinking is, if you eat it because you don't want to "waste" it, then you'll just carry the extra weight with you as opposed to dumping it in the garbage. Either way, the food is wasted.

Of course, I would certainly advise you to take precautions against wasting food. And you can always save your leftovers for later. However, it is important to get used to not finishing everything on your plate, too, since it will take some time to learn how to accurately judge how much food is best for you to consume at one sitting. One solution is to put less on your plate to begin with. When serving yourself food, be mindful of how much food you're taking, and always give yourself less rather than more. After all, you can always serve yourself extra if you discover you are still hungry!

The challenge for you is that other people will become confused or even upset when they see you eating smaller portions or leaving over some of your meal. People often feel good when they can offer food to others, especially guests. It will take a belief in yourself and the application of everything you will have learned in this program that will allow you to follow your own course and refuse to be swayed by others' expectations of you (due to their own food and eating issues).

After the meal

Once you've finished eating, it is preferable to wait five minutes before you engage in another activity. This gives your digestive system even more time to do its job effectively before blood and oxygen get re-directed to someplace else in your body.

After eating, pay attention to how you feel. This information is invaluable, since it will give you feedback about what is right and not so right for your body and its well-being. Asking yourself the following questions can be quite useful. One of the best ways to record this information is by keeping a food diary:

- o   Time of day and location
- o   What you ate
- o   Does your body react to the food in a particular way?
- o   Does the food enhance or drain your energy?
- o   How is your mood after the meal?
- o   How did you feel one hour after eating?
- o   How did you feel the next morning?
- o   Did you notice any physical symptoms after the meal (such as burping, gas or cramps)?

- Did you notice any physical symptoms the following day (for example, skin breaking out)?
- What does your intuition tell you about whether this food is right for you or not?

The "What" of Eating

Eating is the most intimate thing a person can do...the food you eat actually becomes a part of you! Plus, anything you ingest will create various chemical reactions within your body. This means that each thing you eat will have an effect on you, both physically and mentally. Your goal is to pay attention to how different foods affect you, and then choose accordingly. By following *The Buddha Diet*, you will naturally gravitate towards foods that make you feel good and give you positive energy, and avoid foods which make you feel bad. As mentioned above, a food diary is a great way to keep track of how particular foods and meals affect your physical and mental states of being. This means what you eat is not going to be based on specific dietary guidelines or a restrictive regimen. Rather, it is based on noticing how you feel after you've eaten: immediately following a meal, the hours afterwards, and even the next day. By keeping a food diary, you will be able to easily spot patterns so that you can modify what and how you eat. Therefore, no food is off-limits – unless **you** want it to be.

Personally, the way I decide whether or not to eat something is to ask myself, "Is this food clogging or cleansing?" Intuitively, I know the answer immediately.

And so will you! The key is to honor the choices we know truly serve our best interests. Developing the ability to do so is the focus of the remainder of this book.

As I mentioned above, *The Buddha Diet* is based on intuitive eating: Nothing is off-limits. When and how you eat is more important than what you eat. However, since knowledge is power, you might be interested in considering the following information:

- Protein and high fiber foods are very satisfying nutrients (both empty out of the stomach slowly). Simple sugars are least satisfying because they empty from the stomach very quickly. Interestingly, fat is very satisfying because it empties from the stomach most slowly. The problem, however, is that we tend to keep eating fat past satiation....

- Pay attention to your caffeine intake – it is a powerful drug.

- Notice your white sugar intake – it is also a powerful drug.

- Consider your consumption of processed foods – they contain many synthetic chemicals that can deeply affect your body.

- Be curious about food labels, so you can be informed about what you are putting into your body.

- It is easier to digest warm foods compared to cold foods, especially in the morning.

o It is also easier to digest cooked or steamed foods than raw foods.

o We are often allergic to the foods which we crave...

o Pay attention to your water intake. When you feel hungry, it is usually because you are thirsty! Water is important because it:
    o Maintains blood pressure and flow
    o Digests the food you eat
    o Transports nutrients throughout your body
    o Eliminates waste products from your body
    o Decreases constipation
    o Protects and lubricates your organs and tissues
    o Regulates and maintains your body temperature
    o Metabolizes fat
    o Gives a feeling of fullness

• Consider your breakfast foods and how you eat them.
    o First of all, have breakfast! You've been sleeping all night and it's time to break your fast – this is a vital meal that will give you energy for the rest of the morning.
    o Notice how you are balancing protein and carbohydrates, along with fats. A balanced combination of all three ensures a steady supply of energy throughout the morning.
    o See if you can detect a difference in how you feel after eating a warm meal at breakfast, such as oatmeal, versus a cold one, such as cereal with milk.

- Consider your pace of eating breakfast – are you rushing or eating in your car? Or are you able to relax while you eat?
- Experiment with drinking water (at room-temperature) first thing in the morning at least a half hour before you eat. See how this helps to regulate your bowel movements and increase your energy.

- Pay attention to those foods that hold your blood sugar steady and don't cause you to feel lethargic after an initial burst of energy.

***

Now that you have an idea of what a healthy relationship with food and eating looks like, what might stop you from changing your habits? Remember, you can't rely on will-power. And you shouldn't have to. Instead, it will be your self-love and commitment to your own well-being that will always steer you in the right direction.

So how to avoid sabotaging yourself? This is where the rest of the book comes in. Like anything else you wish to master, your familiarity and comfort with the following eight skills will grow in proportion to the time you spend practicing them. With enough effort, they will become like second nature!

Chapter 4

Skill #1: Mindfulness

Question: *What one word should I carry with me for the rest of my life?*

        Peter Bloom

Answer: *Observation!*

        Milton Erickson

The moment one gives close attention to anything, even a blade of grass, it becomes a mysterious, awesome, indescribably magnificent world in itself.

    Henry Miller

Facing the bluntness of reality is the highest form of sanity and enlightened vision....Devotion proceeds through various stages of unmasking until we reach the point of seeing the world directly and simply without imposing our fabrications...

    Chogyam Trungpa Rinpoche

One of his students asked the Buddha, "Are you the messiah?" "No," answered the Buddha. "Then are you a healer?" "No," the Buddha replied. "Then are you a teacher?" the student persisted. "No, I am not a teacher." "Then what are you?" asked the student, exasperated. "I am awake," the Buddha replied.

Mindfulness is a cornerstone of Buddhist philosophy. I have included this skill because it greatly influences what we choose to eat, the manner in which we eat it, and how much we consume. Approaching food and eating with mindfulness will have an immense impact on your ability to manage your weight and feel good about what you put into your body. I also want to introduce this skill first because it will allow you to be successful with the other seven.

But what exactly does "mindfulness" entail?

The concept of mindfulness includes the ideas of:

- Awareness of the present moment
- Focused attention
- Acceptance

Working with mindfulness, you will consider *where* you place our attention, and *how* you go about doing things. As you practice this skill, you will learn that instead of being trapped in the past or future, you can access a sense of freedom that can only be experienced by living in the present. This is because when it comes to reality, the present moment is where health and healing are to be found. The "**now**" is where spontaneity, acceptance, and compassion live. It is the space in which you are able to take deliberate action for your own benefit.

We have little control over the past or the future. However, we often base our decision-making on prior experiences or expectations about the future. Indeed, things that happened to us in the past generally influence how we experience the present (and think about the future). Our beliefs, ideals, self-images, memories, desires, hopes, prejudices, attitudes, assumptions, and accumulated knowledge all combine to create the lens through which we see – and interact with – ourselves and the world around us. And that lens colors our response to everything that we experience. The result is that we lose the ability to respond appropriately to situations as they arise. Instead of being able to act spontaneously, our past conditioning greatly limits our choices in the present.

We can break these chains to the past, however, when we become aware of our current thoughts, feelings, and body sensations.

Through mindfulness, we gain freedom, as we realize a type of clarity that allows us to see things as they are, not as we fear or hope they are. From this we then can create authentic and meaningful connections with what is happening around us. And that is vital, because we can create change only in the present moment.

So a major goal of mindfulness is to develop the ability to see things as they really are, uninfluenced by our past conditioning. By acting deliberately instead of reactively, we can experience ourselves spontaneously in the moment, as we get in touch with our true, essential nature. But in order to do that, we must first become conscious of how we avoid being present in our daily life. This means gaining an understanding of how our past conditioning constrains our choices in the present. As we become students of our own minds, we can use the knowledge we gain to escape our habitual reactions, thereby freeing ourselves to make appropriate responses in life.

At the same time, we can use our mindfulness skills to notice how often we become disengaged from what is going on around us. It is easy to be distracted. Our pace of life usually is fast and we are often forced to multitask. Instead of fully being in the present moment, we are in multiple places at once. By checking in with ourselves and noticing that we are not present, we can recognize what is happening. That knowledge then allows us shift our attention back to what is happening right in front of us.

This is especially true about food and eating. Think about how often you actually pay close attention to the process of choosing, preparing and eating food. It is easy to eat an entire meal and not really taste even a single bite! It is also easy to prepare and eat an entire meal based not on true feelings of hunger, but rather on habit.

But when you begin to pay close attention to what you are putting on your plate and into your mouth, you will experience a connection with food and eating that will be both empowering and satisfying. Instead of being an unconscious process, it will become meaningful. And when you notice how your body feels after a meal, you will gain important information about how food truly affects you.

I have divided the idea of mindfulness into is six main components. With each description, I offer ideas for how to integrate it into your life. Remember, your commitment to learning this skill is an investment in the quality of the rest of your life!

Paying attention

This is a core aspect of mindfulness. To pay attention means *slowing down* enough so that you are able to notice what is going on around you. It means committing to a pace that is the opposite of *rushing*. And as you slow yourself down and move deliberately through your life, all you need to do is observe your surroundings. Sounds simple, doesn't it? But this is a way of living that many of us are divorced from, because our minds usually are "somewhere else."

The easiest way to tap into this aspect of mindfulness is to pay attention to each of your senses. Shift your focus to what you **see** around you. What you **hear**. How things **feel** to your body. When you are eating, notice the texture of your food, both in your hands and in your mouth. Be attentive to what you **taste** and how it **smells**. And then focus on how you feel after your meal.

Paying attention also means focusing on what is going on inside of you throughout the day. Notice how you are breathing. Where in your chest is your breath? Is it deep or shallow? Observe your mood and any emotions you might be experiencing. What are you feeling? If you notice that you are not in the present moment, then where are you? Thinking about the past? Imagining the future? Are you distracted? How so? Why?

The most important thing you can do with this skill is to notice – and be curious about – where your attention goes. Curiosity is a wonderful characteristic; pretend you are a stranger observing yourself, who is interested in why you are doing what you are doing. This will give you all the information you need about your current state of being. And once you begin to recognize unhelpful patterns, then you can begin to change. This is especially true with your relationship with food. As you start to discover the connection between your attention and how you eat, you will discover a lot about yourself. It is this feedback which will enable you to make more informed decisions about your eating process. In addition, your ability to pay attention will allow you to effectively utilize The Hunger Scale. Once you begin paying attention to your sense of physical hunger and fullness, you will be able to know exactly when to start and stop eating.

Tip: If you find that you are distracted and are having a difficult time focusing attention on yourself or your surroundings, try one of the following ideas to help re-orient yourself:

o Notice what is *directly* in front of you and pay attention to it.
o Pick one of your five senses and focus especially on it.
o Notice your breath and follow it as you inhale and exhale.
o Pick a part of your body and really pay attention to it. For example, notice your hand or your fingers.

o Tell yourself, either out-loud or silently, "Focus!" or "Slow down!"

Concentration

This form of mindfulness refers to committing one's attention directly to whatever task is at hand. Connected to the skill of paying attention, this refers to the ability to filter out distractions, and be completely present while engaged in doing something. The idea of focusing on one thing at a time may sound easy, but as I mentioned above, our pace of life often makes this difficult to put into practice.

When you develop the skill of concentration, you will find that you will be able to truly inhabit the present moment. Some people refer to this as being in the "zone," where time actually stands still. When we eat, it is very easy to be distracted. If we are eating and reading, watching TV, or thinking about other things, we often become disconnected from what we are putting into our bodies. This lack of connection means we are unaware of exactly what we are eating and how much we are consuming. Paying attention to that process and concentrating on each bite of food will give you control over this important part of your life.

Tip: The best way to develop your capacity for paying attention and concentration is through **meditation**. There are several ways to meditate. In one kind of meditation practice, the goal is to focus on a single thing while sitting comfortably in a place where you won't be disturbed. For example, you can simply follow your breath in and out. Or you can choose a word like "love" or "peace" and silently repeat it over and over in your mind or out loud. You could also use any stationary object (like a flower, a bowl, or even a spot on the wall) as your focal point.

My recommendation is to buy a digital timer so you don't have to worry about keeping track of time while you meditate. (I keep mine under a pillow next to me so the alarm isn't jarring). Then start out by meditating for two minutes at a set time each day. As you begin to feel more comfortable and confident in your ability to stay focused, you can slowly start to add time to your meditation experience. When I was beginning my own practice, I started out meditating two minutes each afternoon. Because I found that short amount of time so do-able, I could never come up with an excuse not to meditate! Then I simply added one minute per day until I reached twenty minutes, which became my set time.

The goal is for you to leave your meditative state feeling relaxed and refreshed. If you find that you're becoming sleepy or are losing your concentration, then stick with a shorter time. Remember to feel free to experiment. I believe that even two minutes of meditation practice each day is better than none at all.

As an added bonus, research has proven that a regular meditation practice can lead to better sleep, stress reduction, improved mental health, lowered blood pressure and a whole host of other health benefits!

Another option for strengthening your ability to be mindful is to focus on a chore, like washing the dishes or folding laundry. The key is to choose something and then practice directing your attention to it. If you find that your attention wanders, all you need to do is notice what is happening, and then gently bring your focus back to what you were originally concentrating on. You can also develop this skill by making a commitment to practice it with each meal, since you will have that opportunity multiple times each day.

Witness consciousness

This aspect of mindfulness refers to the capacity to notice your thoughts and feelings without becoming caught up in them. It is as though you are an outside observer objectively watching what is happening in your mind. You can access witness consciousness by paying attention to your thoughts and emotions as they arise – and then noticing as they dissipate and are replaced by new ones. In this way, witness consciousness will give you a broad perspective of yourself as you realize that there is more to you than just the thoughts and feelings that you experience.

The sensation of being a curious, objective observer of your inner workings will allow you to recognize that you do not have to get completely consumed by what you are thinking or feeling. It demonstrates that there is a part of you that is of a more essential nature, and that what you are observing, as much as it might feel permanent in that moment, is actually transitory. Tapping into your witness consciousness also gives you the power to learn about the patterns of thinking that cause you pain. As you become familiar with your mental process, and discover when and where certain thought patterns occur, you can use your self-knowledge to short-circuit habitual, automatic responses that are unhelpful.

When it comes to food, you can use your witness consciousness to observe your mental and emotional states as you make a decision about what and how to eat. You will be able to tell yourself, "I am aware that I'm angry and that I am thinking that what happened at work is unfair. I also notice that I am craving cookies right now. I know that I am not hungry for food, but I still want to eat because I believe that eating those cookies will make me feel better." This kind of conversation with yourself will certainly be new and different if you are used to dealing with a distressing feeling by simply going for food, without thinking about it. As you learn to pay close attention to what you are feeling and the thoughts going through your head, you will be able to make important connections. In this case, you can clearly see that your desire to eat cookies is connected with feeling stressed. That knowledge buys you time, since you can step back and ask yourself, "Since I know that I want to eat those cookies because I am upset, not because I am hungry, is this a good choice for me? Is there some other way to deal with this stress that doesn't involve doing something I know I'll regret immediately afterwards?"

Tip: This kind of mental distance is especially helpful when you have a thought or feeling that begins with "I am ---." For example, you might think to yourself, "I am scared to get on that plane." Or, "I am stupid for making that mistake." This language is dangerous, because the verb "I am" refers to an enduring reality, and makes no allowance for the fact that your feelings and thoughts represent only one aspect of who you are, and temporarily at that.

So rather than thinking "I am scared to get on the plane," you can tell yourself, "**I am having the feeling of** being scared…" Or if you notice that you're thinking to yourself, "I'm stupid", you can instead rephrase it as, "**I am having the thought** that I am stupid." Although a bit awkward, this kind of phrasing has two advantages. First, it will remind you that instead of being permanent, these thoughts and feelings are actually passing phases. Second, your witness consciousness allows you to recognize the inner workings of your thinking and feeling process. This in turn leads to empowerment, because once you understand that your thoughts are not facts, but instead are messages you are giving yourself, then you can take a step back and decide exactly how seriously to take those messages, and what to do about them. I'll talk more about how to do that in the chapter on how to overcome irrational thinking.

Holding thoughts lightly

The Buddhist concept of *nonattachment* refers to the idea that everything is temporary. We suffer when we believe that something is permanent and therefore become attached to it. Such clinging only leads to pain because everything in life is transitory. This not only includes things and people, but thoughts as well. We often become distressed when we focus on a particular thought. We go over it endlessly in our mind, repeating it over and over. In psychology we refer to this as "*rumination.*" When it refers to a cow (its original meaning) rumination means that the animal is re-chewing something that has already been chewed slightly and swallowed. Now for a person, that process is unnatural. After all, once we chew and swallow something, our body is supposed to process and eliminate it. But when it comes to worrying, we often keep thoughts swirling in our heads without letting them go. Dwelling continually on negative thoughts often leads to non-hungry eating, as we then use food to soothe distressing feelings. This is why understanding and utilizing the skill of nonattachment is so vital.

By making a commitment to holding our thoughts lightly we remind ourselves that they are not actual, enduring facts. This type of mindfulness practice will help you avoid becoming entangled in your thinking. By committing to simply noticing the thoughts and images coming up for you in your mind, you will soon realize that they are part of a never-ending stream. Like clouds in the sky, they come and then soon go. Even the most distressing thoughts, such as "This is hopeless" or "I'll never be able to do this right" eventually dissipate and give way to new thoughts – if you let that process occur naturally. In that sense, ruminating on a thought keeps you trapped in a negative feedback loop. Or perhaps it is more accurate to say that rumination leads into a downward spiral, as the more time you spend running around in a mental circle, the more distressed you will become. Consider the following Buddhist parable:

A senior monk and a junior monk were travelling together. At one point, they came to a river with a strong current. As the monks were preparing to cross the river, they saw a young and beautiful woman also attempting to cross. The young woman asked if they could help her.

The senior monk carried the woman on his shoulder, forded the river and set her down on the other bank. The junior monk seemed upset, but said nothing.

They both continued walking. Sometime later the senior monk noticed that his junior was particularly quiet and asked "Is something the matter? You seem upset."

The junior monk replied, "As monks, we are not permitted any contact with women, certainly not physical contact. How could you carry that woman on your shoulders?" The senior monk smiled and said, "That's interesting....I left the woman at the bank of the river a long time ago. You, however, seem to be still carrying her."

Tip #1: You can become skilled at this type of mindfulness through a certain type of meditation. This particular practice consists of sitting quietly in a space where you won't be disturbed. When you are settled, close your eyes and allow your mind to be open to all of the thoughts that pass through it. At the same time, permit your body to be open to all of the feelings that it experiences. Instead of focusing on a single thing, just let your thoughts arise naturally. The key is to let the thoughts come and go without attaching energy and attention to them. Don't dwell on them. Don't judge them. Simply be open to whatever arises. Notice what you are thinking. Observe what comes up. But then allow new thoughts and feelings to follow. Just observe what this experience is like.

Tip #2: If you find that your anxiety is interfering with your ability to let go of your thoughts, here is an idea that works for some people. Schedule thirty minutes per day that you will dedicate solely to worrying. When anxious thoughts come up outside of those thirty minutes, tell yourself that those thoughts can go away and wait for their scheduled time, during which you can ruminate on them all you want! I have found that those thoughts often do respond to your request...

Acceptance

This aspect of mindfulness is the acknowledgment of things that are happening to us – without trying to analyze, resist, or change them. By practicing acceptance, we commit ourselves to be fully present with whatever we are feeling and experiencing. No clinging. No rejecting. One of the Buddha's major teachings is that by resisting or struggling with an uncomfortable experience, we actually increase our suffering. This is because when we ignore or disown our thoughts, emotions, and sensations, we are actually ignoring or disowning a part of ourselves. After all, if you are thinking or feeling something, then it is legitimate on some level. So the key is not to deny something you are thinking or feeling. Rather, the solution lays in what you do decide to do with those thoughts and feelings. Do you ruminate over them, or let them take their natural course?

Acceptance consists of releasing our expectations about how we would like things to happen in our lives. Because the outcome is often out of our control, all we can do is try our best in each present moment. It is true that we often wish the present moment were different than the way it is.

However, we will only find peace by accepting what is out of our control. Indeed, you may find that the moment you accept that which you have been resisting, your relationship to it will change – for the better.

Tip: The best way I know how to become clear about my control (or lack thereof) over reality is through **The Serenity Prayer**. The author of the prayer is thought to be the Protestant theologian Reinhold Niebuhr, who composed it in the early 1940s. Think of it as a guiding light when you have to make a decision about where to focus your energy.

> **God grant me the serenity**
> **to accept the things I cannot change;**
> **the courage to change the things I can;**
> **and the wisdom to know the difference.**

We can access that "wisdom to know the difference" by taking the time to ask ourselves what is truly possible or impossible in a given situation. And then, based on the answer, we can either take the appropriate action or make peace with what is. Both choices require the courage to feel discomfort. But that discomfort is temporary, as opposed to the permanent suffering we experience when we are mistaken about the power we do or don't have in our lives. This aspect of mindfulness will come in handy when you practice overcoming emotional eating (explained in more detail in chapter ten).

Acceptance as non-judgment

Acceptance also means acknowledging something without judging it. By going into our heads and labeling something as "good" or "bad" we prevent ourselves from experiencing it fully. Wishing something were different than it actually is, we cause ourselves frustration and distress. This of course can lead to emotional eating, which is why this aspect of mindfulness is important. So non-judgment is accepting something as it is, without overlaying our preference one way or another onto it. After all, when you fight with reality and focus on the way you wish things *would* or *could* be, you will only end up banging your head against a very tough wall. Now this doesn't necessarily mean that it is OK when bad things happen to you. As you will learn in chapter eleven, there are strategies you can learn to make peace with reality without approving of it.

To practice this skill, simply notice the evaluations you make about yourself and others. When you are tempted to criticize or judge yourself, you must remember that you are doing the best you can. And when you evaluate others, it helps to do so with a sense of compassion, as it is impossible to know the real reasons behind other people's actions. This does not mean unconditional acceptance of behavior that harms others. Instead, this form of mindfulness asks you to consider that a person always makes the best choice they can, given their view of the world. A person's choice may be self-defeating, strange or hurtful, but for them it seems the best choice at the time. The key is to acknowledge the positive intention of the other person's behavior. However, for the purposes of *The Buddha Diet*, I would like you to focus on how, when, and why you judge yourself (more on this in chapters four through six).

In order to develop this skill, pay attention to how often you make judgments. What do you notice happens in your body when you judge or complain? Do you feel any tightness? What happens to your mood? What if you replaced your judgmental stance with a sense of detached curiosity? How might that make you feel?

As I mentioned above, when we wish something weren't the way it is, we are actually fighting with reality. And that is a fight we can never win. For example, if I forget to buy milk, I can berate myself for being stupid and forgetful. But that doesn't change the fact that the milk was forgotten. It is more helpful to recognize that I forgot to buy milk and then ask myself what I now need to do about it. In doing so, I now have created an opportunity to treat myself more gently. Even if I still have the judgmental thought, I can observe that I am having the thought, that I am doing the best I can in the moment, and then let it go. That's the beauty of being nonjudgmental; all the negative messages we're used to telling ourselves are suddenly cut off and the ensuing compassion creates the possibility of inner peace.

Tip: It is difficult to live without making judgments. Our preferences for things fill our heads constantly as we go about our day. So don't be hard on yourself if you find it is hard to be judgment-free. Rather, I believe the benefit from this skill occurs if you simply observe a judgment when it arises in your mind, note that it is occurring, and then let the thought move away. One key is avoid ruminating on the judgment. Another key is to remember that a judgment is not a fact. A final suggestion is that when you find yourself making a judgment, you can ask yourself a simple question: "Is this helpful?" Your answer will help you decide whether or not it is beneficial for you to focus on that train of thought.

***

As you practice the skill of mindfulness – in all of its aspects – your relationship with food can't help but change. In particular, as you work to develop this skill, I would like you to begin paying close attention to two things: your stomach and your energy level. By remembering to focus on your physical body and the messages it is sending you about food, you will be able to cultivate a relationship with eating that is truly healthy and healing. Use your mindfulness abilities to check in with yourself throughout the day, and during your meals, to determine where you are on the Hunger Scale. To review from the last chapter, here it is again:

The Hunger Scale:

- o Starving
- o Ravenous
- o Hungry
- o Slightly hungry
- o No feeling in stomach; satisfaction
- o Mildly full; slightly feeling the food in your stomach
- o Full; feeling the food fully in your stomach
- o Uncomfortably full
- o Stuffed; feeling sick

Your goal is to eat when you feel hungry and then to stop eating **before** you feel any fullness in your stomach. And the only way to do that is to become mindful of your stomach! ***This means slowing down and paying attention.*** It might take you a while to learn how to recognize your own personal sense of hunger and satisfaction, but this is a worthwhile endeavor because it means you are interested in honoring your body's true needs. Doing so will cause you to feel better, both physically and emotionally.

You will also notice that the more mindful you are during your meals, the less food you will consume. We often overestimate how much food we need to eat; being mindful will allow you to discover how much is really enough. And typically that is not as much as you think!

So what will you do if you want to eat for a reason other than physical hunger? Don't worry – that is subject of chapters ten and eleven. For now, simply direct your attention to rediscovering what it really feels like to be physically hungry and physically satisfied. Each and every day you will have countless opportunities to practice!

The several next chapters in The Buddha Diet will assist you in changing your current relationship with yourself. As you learn how to truly understand who you are and why you are worthy of your own unconditional love and acceptance, you will find it easier to treat yourself with kindness. I will begin with your value system, and how it influences your motivation "to do the right thing.

Chapter 5

Skill #2: Accessing Authentic Values

Your soul suffers if you live superficially.

Albert Schweitzer

And the day came when the risk it took to remain tight inside the bud was more than the risk it took to blossom.

Anais Nin

Your work is to discover your world and then with all your heart give yourself to it.

the Buddha

It takes courage to grow up and become who you really are.

e.e. cummings

By creating a connection with your deepest values, you will lay the foundation for success in future change, especially with food and eating. Being clear and comfortable about who you are and what you stand for will allow you to develop the motivation and commitment necessary for changing. Most importantly, being aligned with your true values automatically gives you the ability to make *the* right choice when you are faced with a decision about ***anything***. This is why your decision-making process about what, when and how to eat will eventually feel effortless. By using the mindfulness skills you just learned, you will be able to connect with your deepest values in the present moment, and from there instantly know how to proceed.

In turn, how and what you eat will give you the energy you need to pursue the life that really matters to you!

What exactly are "values"?

Values are personal beliefs about what is good and bad, or right and wrong. They are also ideas about what is important to us in life. We typically want more of what we value in our lives and less of what we do not. Accordingly, our values point us in particular directions and steer us away from others. Some of the values we hold are situational, and apply to specific times, contexts, or people. Other values are much more core to who we are and transcend any specific situation. They guide us across all the domains of our lives. These core values determine the people and opportunities we seek out, and the ones we avoid. They shape the goals we set in life, and then motivate us to move toward those goals. Ultimately, they are the standards we use to evaluate our own actions and the actions of others.

Examples of values: Balance; community; family; adventure; safety; affluence; calmness; friendship; discipline; work; honesty; faith; solitude; charity; learning; relaxation; health; thrift; playfulness; athleticism.

Core values lead to clear intentions, which then point the way to committed actions. Think about it: People who are the same way on the inside as they are on the outside are truly aligned. There is no dissonance between what they feel and how they act. They have **integrity,** which comes from the Latin word *integer*, meaning "one."

When we are connected to values that deeply resonate with us, change comes naturally. That is, when our values are guiding us, our decision-making process becomes effortless. There simply isn't a question of what to do, since following our values makes it immediately clear which course to follow. This might be challenging, since we sometimes we have to spend time around people whose values are in conflict with our own. But the knowledge that your actions are aligned with what you truly believe can be its own source of strength.

Where do values come from?

Values aren't something we are born with. Instead, we learn them as we grow up. Value systems are influenced by our childhood environment. Parents, peers, school, religious institutions, and the media all send us messages about what is good and bad, acceptable and unacceptable about the world. As children, it is difficult to be critical of such messages. Accordingly, we usually soak up the messages that surround us, or the ones that make an emotional impression on us. **However, it is important to realize that because we have learned them, we can also unlearn them if we discover that our current values do not serve our best interests.**

Where did *your* values come from? The following journal questions will help you understand how your value system was created. You can answer these questions all in one sitting or spread them out over a period of several days. It is important that you take your time with them, and give yourself support if necessary, since they might bring up some upsetting memories.

(Note: I use the words "mother" and "father" in the questions below; if you were raised by a grandparent or some other caretaker, please substitute accordingly).

- Write five adjectives to describe what it was like to grow up in your home.
- Who were the main people in your home environment? Please describe what your relationship was like with each one.
- Which five adjectives would best describe your experience of your mother?
- How did you get along with your mother when you were a child?
- What are five things you learned from your mother (positive or negative)?
- Which five adjectives would best describe your father?

- What kind of relationship did you have with your father when you were a child?
- What were five things you learned from your father (positive or negative)?
- Were your relationships with your mother and father similar? Different? How so?
- What kinds of things did you do together as a family when you were a child?
- When you were a child, did your mother and/or father ever reject you? Can you remember any specific examples? How did you feel when you were rejected? How did you respond?
- When you were a child, how did your care-takers discipline you? Were there ever any punishments that made a strong impression on you? Were there any that you can still vividly remember?
- What kinds of messages did you receive about yourself from your father and mother? What did you learn about your role in life from your parents? Do you feel those messages influenced your life? If so, how?
- When you were a child, did anybody close to you (friend or relative) pass away? Do you remember your experience of that time? Do you remember if you were able to grieve? And if so, how you grieved? Did you receive assistance from anybody in understanding and processing that death?
- As a child, were there people in your life who you could count on for support besides your parents? What were those relationships like?
- During childhood, did you have any coping mechanisms that helped you feel safe when you were threatened, or made you feel better when you

were sad, anxious or upset? Are any of these coping mechanisms still present in your life as an adult? Do they still work? Are there any negative side effects?

- Was your family religious? Were there certain ideas and rules about life that you learned from your religious tradition?
- What do you remember about images you watched on television or in the movies? Did any of those disturb you or make you feel badly about yourself? Which ones? Why?
- Do you remember any books or magazines that made an impression on you while you were growing up? Why do you think they made an impression? What did you learn about yourself from them? What did you learn about the world around you?

Based on the answers to the above questions, what do you now know about how your concept of yourself – and the world around you – was created? Do you believe that the experiences you had growing up may have influenced the decisions you made later in life? Have you discovered any evidence that how you think and feel about yourself and the world today as an adult is connected to your childhood experiences?

It is important that you understand that you weren't born knowing good from bad. You learned those standards while growing up as you received messages from the people and institutions in your life. It can be quite empowering to recognize that those standards – those values – were learned. Which means that you can adjust them if necessary.

Now it is time to focus on your current values. Think back to the definition of "values" from above. These are ways of being that are important to you, that resonate with your soul. Examples can be things such as family, achievement, adventure, or solitude. Other values could be: never quitting, always being there for others, or not showing anger.

You will begin to articulate your own values by numbering 1-25 on a blank piece of paper. On the top of the page, write the heading, "**This is important to me in how I live my life**." Now fill in as many of the 25 spaces as you are able. It doesn't matter what you write or how you write it, just as long as it is recognizable as a "value."

When you are done, copy down your answers onto a separate piece of paper, but now also include **why** each is important to you.

After you have finished, take a break for at least an hour (a day is better). When you feel refreshed, come back to your list of values. Take some time to look them over. Notice how you feel in your gut when you read what you have written. You may end up discarding some of your current values because you can now recognize that they don't serve your best interests. Others you may decide to keep. The following part of this exercise will assist you in making those decisions. Once again, take your time with this. It is perfectly fine to break it up over several days or over the course of a week.

For each of the values that you have listed, please read and then think about the following statements. Use your answers to help you determine whether to keep or discard each of your values.

- I have chosen this value consciously and deliberately
- I know how and why this value became important to me
- This is a core part of who I am
- Without this value I would be a different person
- My life is aligned around this value
- My future goals are connected to this value
- This value resonates deeply within me
- This value empowers me
- This value can cause me to feel badly about myself
- This value has led to situations which I later regreted
- I always notice this value in other people
- I very much want to have this value in my life
- When this value is threatened, I feel emotional pain
- I feel satisfied when I am actively expressing this value in my life
- Every day, I am able to express this value in some manner
- I have made sacrifices for the sake of this value
- I am attracted to people and situations that also have this value

You might notice that some of your values bring you peace or fulfillment. Others may cause you suffering or conflict. It's good that you are noticing; I want you to become conscious of how your values have impacted – and continue to impact – the quality of your life.

This is a powerful time of transition. You have the chance now, as an adult, to consciously create a value system that will serve your higher good. Therefore it is natural that you will have some values that you know you would like to keep, while there are others that you would like to release. It is vital to remember that this process will bring about a change in you as a person. As you readjust your value system, you are becoming a different person than you were before. This may create anxiety, because you are entering new territory. Therefore, it may be helpful for you to think about how to mourn the values that you are leaving behind. After all, they were part of your life for a long time.

Saying "Good-bye" to a value

The most important thing to remember when you release a value that no longer serves you is that you learned it from someone or somewhere else – you weren't born with it. At the time you learned it, it seemed necessary. Force may have been involved, or perhaps it was appealing on some other level. But once you recognize that you have the power to let a value go, you can imagine that, like a snake, you are shedding skin that you have outgrown. And that's OK. You can silently wish that value a "good-bye" and remind yourself that it doesn't have to guide your decisions anymore. You now know that there are other, more empowering ways to lead your life.

Because this is an in-between, transitional, time for you, it is especially important to recognize and honor this process of releasing and becoming. By making peace with what was formerly important to you, and understanding why it is in your best interests to leave certain values behind, you will clear the path for new growth as you move forward. The challenge you have is being willing to trust your intuition as it guides you to a way of grieving for the values you are leaving behind. Those values were once a very deep part of you. And as the author William Bridges notes, "You have to make an ending before you make a beginning."

"Transition does not require that you reject or deny the importance of your old life, just that you let go of it. Far from rejecting it, you are likely to do better with the ending if you honor the old life for all that it did for you. It got you this far. It brought you everything you have. But now – although it may be some time before you are comfortable actually doing so – it is time for you to let go of it. Your old life is over. No matter how much you would like to continue it or rescue it or fix it, it's time to let it go." (William Bridges)

*"Transition **renews** us. It is as though the breakdown of the old reality releases energy that has been trapped in the form of our old lives and converts it back into its original state of pure and formless energy."* (William Bridges)

When you feel ready, it will be time to continue your search for other empowering values to add to the ones you already have. The journal questions below will give you a chance to search out and reconnect with important parts of yourself that perhaps have been buried or denied since childhood. Now is the time to get in touch with what is truly important to you, what makes you feel alive, having a life worth living.

As you consciously create a value-system based on your own (not somebody else's) standards, you will set in place a way of looking at the world – and being in it – which will feel "right" to you. It will feel honest. You will feel comfortable owning it. When you can stand in the certainty of who are as a person, knowing in your bones what you stand for and what you believe in, then you will be able to access the motivation and commitment to follow a path of positive change, especially when it comes to food and eating.

Journal questions

By answering the following questions, you will gain important insights about yourself that perhaps you have forgotten or are unconscious of. This information will allow you to make additions to your list of core values.

Just to let you know upfront, the large number of questions you'll be answering might make you feel you've entered a values-generating boot camp! So be easy on yourself and take your time. There is no rush. By giving each question the consideration it deserves, you will be presenting yourself with a powerful gift.

- Think back to when you were a child. What did you want to be when you grew up? What was it about your choice(s) that made you feel excited?
- When you were young, did you have one or more favorite television shows? What were they? What was it about them that made an impression on you?

- Growing up, did you have a favorite book? What was it about that book that resonated with you?
- What was your favorite movie as a child? Why? What about now, as an adult?

- In your past, what have you been an example of? How did that make you feel?
- Currently, what are you an example of? How does that make you feel?

- What does it mean to be alive?

- Describe a time when you felt that you were truly alive.

- What brings tears to your eyes?

- If time and money were not an issue, what would you do with your life? What would your days look like?

- If you had one year to live, how would you spend it?
- If you had one month to live, how would you spend it?

- Happiness is (use 7 sentences):
- Happiness is (use 7 words):
- Now pick just one word – Happiness is:

- What would you like to do someday?

- Describe a time in your life when you felt that you were doing what you were born to do.

- List ten wishes.

- What is your wildest dream?

- What would make your life perfect?

- Ideally, where would you like to be in your life five years from now?
    - What are you doing now that will lead to that?
    - What are you doing now that will keep you from that?

- What do you believe is the meaning of life?
- What is the meaning of your particular life?
- What matters to you?
- Who would you like to serve in your life? To whom would you like to make a difference?

- Think of three people (past or present) who you respect and admire. For each of these people, list three qualities which resonate with you.

- Currently, where is your time going? How are you spending it?
- How would you ideally like to be using your time?

- What are you tolerating in your life?
- Which people/places/things drain you of energy?
- Which people/places/things give you energy?
- What fascinates you?

- Imagine you are an old person, looking back on your life.
    - About what did you worry way too much?
    - What do you wish you had done less of? More of?

- Imagine that you are on your death bed. You have lived a long life. Answer the following question: "What was it that made your life worth living?"

- What will allow you to die without regrets?
- What would the epitaph on your gravestone say?
- If you were to write an obituary for yourself, how would it read?
- You are on your deathbed. What were the three most important lessons you learned in your life? Describe why each one was important.
- In the end, what did you stand for?

So at this point, what have you discovered about who you "really" are? What do you now know is **truly** important to you?

Go back to the original list you made of your core values. What would you add or subtract? What are the factors would you like to have guiding the decisions you make in life?

Mission Statement Exercise

Now I would like you to create what is commonly known as a "mission statement." This is a piece of writing in which you summarize your values and outline what you feel your purpose in life is. It can also include your aspirations and what you would like to achieve in the future. Your wording, the tone, and the length of your mission statement are all up to you. There certainly are plenty of possibilities. Just make sure that what you write resonates deeply within you!

Think of your mission statement as your "personal constitution" or philosophy of life. Creating a personal mission statement provides you with clarity because it defines in writing who you are and how you have decided to live your life. It also succinctly codifies what is important to you and is an easily accessed reminder of your priorities.

Your mission statement should uplift you, so please make it a part of your life. You can keep it in your journal or incorporate it into a piece of art or collage. You could also make a small version of it and keep it in your purse or wallet. You could frame it or just tape it to your wall. Or you could stick it on your refrigerator or bathroom mirror. It doesn't matter – just keep it available for inspiration. Since it captures the essence of who you are and who you want to be, make sure you allow it to empower you by having it handy! As the days, weeks and months pass, you will internalize your mission statement, so physical copies won't be as necessary. But remember – as your life changes, it is perfectly fine to go back and change your mission statement. It is not set in stone. So let it evolve as you do!

Note: At this point, your mission statement does not have to focus on food and eating. That will come later in the book.

To give you a sense of the possibilities, I have provided some examples of mission statements.

Example #1:

My one-sentence mission: To live a balanced life in which I look out for the well-being of others while also honoring my own needs.

My detailed personal mission:

Words that describe me: compassionate, loving, spiritual, balanced, curious, adventure-seeking, persistent, dreamer, educator, advocate, self-aware, father, husband.

I am compassionate. I care about others and want to serve their best-interests. I always want to be sure that I can be of service to the best of my abilities.

I am spiritual. I have a daily spiritual practice that connects me to my higher power. This gives me strength.

I am balanced. I always seek to have balance in my life, making sure that on one area in my life overpowers the rest.

I am curious. I love to learn and will never stop being a student.

I am adventurous. I love to travel and will always look for opportunities to have new experiences.

I am deliberate. I avoid rushing and always do my best to take my time with what I do in life.

I am a husband and father. I am dedicated to my family. Every decision I make must take into account the fact that I want to be there for my family.

Example #2:

"Slow down. Simplify. Be kind." (Naomi Judd)

Example #3:

"To inspire, lift and provide tools for change and growth of individuals and organizations throughout the world to significantly increase their performance capability in order to achieve worthwhile purposes through understanding and living principle-centered leadership." (Stephen Covey)

Example #4:

"Let the first act of every morning be to make the following resolve for the day:
I shall not fear anyone on earth.

I shall fear only God.
I shall not bear ill toward anyone.
I shall not submit to injustice from anyone.
I shall conquer untruth by truth.
And in resisting untruth, I shall put up with all suffering"
(Mahatma Gandhi)

And here is one of my favorite mission statements, from the journalist Erma Bombeck. Note the creative way she used to express her values:

"If I had my life to live over, I would have talked less and listened more. I would have invited friends over to dinner even if the carpet was stained and the sofa faded. I would have eaten the popcorn in the 'good' living room and worried much less about the dirt when someone wanted to light a fire in the fireplace. I would have taken the time to listen to my grandfather ramble about his youth. I would never have insisted the car windows be rolled up on a summer day because my hair had just been teased and sprayed. I would have burned the pink candle sculpted like a rose before it melted in storage. I would have sat on the lawn with my children and not worried about grass stains. I would have cried and laughed less while watching television - and more while watching life. I would have shared more of the responsibility carried by my husband. I would have gone to bed when I was sick instead of pretending the earth would go into a holding pattern if I weren't there for the day. I would never have bought anything just because it was practical, wouldn't show soil or was guaranteed to last a lifetime. Instead of wishing away nine months of pregnancy, I'd have cherished every moment and realized that the wonderment growing inside me was the only chance in life to assist God in a miracle. When my kids kissed me impetuously, I would never have said, "Later. Now go get washed up for dinner." There would have been more "I love you's"... More "I'm sorrys" ... But mostly, given another shot at life, I would seize every minute... look at it and really see it ... live it...and never give it back."

Now it's your turn.

The "Power Questions": How to make the right choice every time

Once you have completed your mission statement, you should be clear about the guiding principles of your life. From this point forward, when you are faced with a decision, asking yourself the following values-based questions beforehand will point you in the right direction.

1. Will my decision move me down a path I have defined as fulfilling or will it keep me stuck in the past?
2. Will my decision bring me satisfaction in the long-run or will it produce instant gratification - followed by remorse?
3. Is my decision congruent with my core values or am I doing this to make another person happy?
4. Is my decision based on love or fear?

5. Will my decision give me energy or will it deplete my life force?
6. Will my decision give me an opportunity to grow or will it give me an excuse to rehash old patterns?
7. Will my decision empower me or will it cause me to lose personal power?
8. Is this decision a way for me to be kind to myself or is it a way for me to hurt myself?

Or....Each time you have a decision to make about anything, simply ask yourself:

"Will what I choose move me closer to what is truly important to me or will it separate me?"

Journal Exercise

Finally, consider this: In the past, it is likely that you encountered barriers that prevented you from developing and living the values that were important to you.

- What were those barriers?
- What did you tell yourself that got in the way?
- What emotions might have made it difficult to pursue your core values?
- Which of your behaviors served as obstacles to manifesting and living your core values?
- What might be current barriers?
- What are some strategies you might use to overcome those barriers?

Chapter 6

Skill #3: Cultivating

Self-Compassion

You can search throughout the entire universe for someone who is more deserving of your love and affection than you are yourself, and that person is not to be found anywhere. You yourself, as much as anybody in the entire universe, deserve your love and affection.

the Buddha

The feeling of being valuable – I am a valuable person – is essential to mental health and a cornerstone of self-discipline. It is the direct product of parental love...When one considers oneself valuable one will take care of oneself in all ways that are necessary.

M. Scott Peck

I do not trust people who don't love themselves and yet tell me, 'I love you.' There is an African saying which is: Be careful when a naked person offers you a shirt.

Maya Angelou

So now you know exactly what you stand for and why. But what about liking yourself? How will that influence your relationship with food and eating?

I believe that in order to create lasting, positive change we must first fully accept ourselves as we are. We also have to be willing to accept *where* we are in life. Self-rejection does not support growth. If you like yourself, you will treat yourself kindly. If you believe you have worth, you will not deliberately hurt yourself. This sense of self-compassion is central to teachings of the Buddha, and influences the core philosophy of *The Buddha Diet*: If you care about your body, you will **naturally** choose the foods that are right for it.

It is our responsibility to derive our self-worth from within, not from other people's opinions of us. It becomes our obligation to provide ourselves with nurturance, affection, and recognition, instead of expecting those things from other people.

This section provides an opportunity for you to think about what prevents you from being kind to yourself. In the last chapter you learned about your authentic self and what you stand for. Now it is time to explore topics such as:

- Self-nurturance
- Your needs and how to get them met
- Developing compassion for your body and its digestive system
- Developing self-forgiveness

My hope is that by the end of this chapter, you will feel really, *really* good about yourself. And thus your relationship with food and eating will naturally change.

The key to positive change is making peace with yourself and believing that you are worthy of unconditional love. Learning to love yourself without limits will provide you with a core sense of self-worth that nobody can take away from you. But, as Julia Cameron notes, it is only when we truly believe that we are "precious objects" that we will be kind to ourselves.

The success of *The Buddha Diet* depends on you reaching a point where you feel comfortable treating yourself with compassion. I define self-compassion as a feeling of protective fondness. It means releasing harsh self-judgment. It means recognizing and honoring your inherent worth. It especially means that you are willing to address your own pain in a nurturing, understanding manner. Awakening to self-compassion is what finally led Siddhartha Gautama away from deprivation and towards inner peace. He realized that trying to measure up to the impossible standards he had set for himself by fasting only produced physical weakness and mental fuzziness. Almost before it was too late, Siddhartha finally was able to understand that his poor body did not deserve to be treated that way. Instead, by softening his attitude towards himself, Siddhartha was able to reconnect with a long-forgotten sense of compassion, which then led to him becoming "the Buddha."

A caveat about "self-esteem"

I would like to talk a bit about "self-esteem," since it so often is included in discussions about feeling good about ourselves. The word "esteem" can be defined as "respect and admiration". Significantly, however, it is not something that you're automatically born with. Rather, it is something you have to "build" or work at maintaining.

So how might you build self-esteem? Typically, you do it by strengthening your ego in two ways. First, by having other people validate you ("I feel good about myself because my father said I'm a good artist"). Second, by comparing yourself favorably to others ("I feel good about myself because I won the race").

This leads to the idea that you can "create" self-esteem by achieving goals and being recognized by others as "special." Of course, the flip side to this is that you can also lose your self-esteem if you make a mistake or fail at something. For example, when somebody else gives you positive feedback about something, you feel good about yourself. And when somebody says something negative to or about you, then you will feel bad.

The result is that when you look outside of yourself for self-worth and self-definition, you give your power to people who do not necessarily have your best interests in mind. This external dependence on other people's approval actually makes you powerless – and insecure. Accordingly, self-esteem ebbs and flows depending on how people respond to you based on your actions; it is out of your control. On the other hand, your self-worth is something that is constant because it is based on your inner "being." No outside source can diminish it because it is constant, no matter what happens outside of you.

But how do we connect with self-compassion and our inherent self-worth? How do we reach a point where we really believe that, no matter what, we are "precious objects"?

Learning to recognize your worth

In every aspect of our lives, we are always asking ourselves, How am I of value? What is my worth? Yet I believe that worthiness is our birthright.

Oprah Winfrey

Self-compassion and self-nurturing are connected to your ability to accept who you are. Self-acceptance means:

- Honoring your experiences, and recognizing that you are doing your best, moment by moment.

- Offering yourself unconditional love, exactly as you are.

- Being willing to be gentle and considerate to yourself.

In turn, self-acceptance is dependent on a sense of self-worth. I believe that self-worth is something you are born with, based on the concept that you have value simply because you exist.

You *deserve* to be here because you *are* here.

Having a healthy sense of self-worth means that you are able to appreciate who you are, regardless of your failures and successes. You recognize your weaknesses and limitations, but you do not let that recognition interfere with your desire and ability to care about yourself and wish yourself well.

Having self-worth does not mean that you are arrogant and compare yourself to others in a judgmental way. Rather, it is having the understanding that nobody is perfect and that you deserve to be nice to yourself *simply because you are human.* It is realizing that each human is unique, each human has a basic worth, and that each human has an essence that is worthy of love, no matter what.

Unfortunately, we often lose our sense of self-worth as we encounter people who judge us when we don't live up to their expectations. This often begins with our parents or care-givers. They sometimes (or often) teach us that there are aspects of ourselves that are unacceptable or unlovable. Since we are children and are greatly influenced by the adults in our lives, we take those messages into our hearts. We then carry those beliefs with us into adulthood.

So now is the time to begin to challenge our self-judgments. It is easy to look back and criticize ourselves for the decisions we have made in our lives. It is easy to be disappointed or frustrated with ourselves. That is why it is important to remember that we make the choices we do in each moment based on what we are aware of and what we are capable of. After all, if we could have done things differently, we would have! When we recognize that we are doing our best with what we have, then we can relax our judgmental stance and instead offer ourselves gentle acceptance.

It is important for you to create your own message for yourself about what it means to be human. Your philosophy should allow you to connect with a sense of unconditional love. For example, you could tell yourself:

"I am a human being. I am not perfect. It is not fair for other people to expect that I be perfect. I am doing my best with what I have moment by moment. That is all I can expect of myself. And in doing so, I love and accept myself as I am."

The following journal exercises will assist you in re-connecting with your inherent self-worth. They are designed to give you the opportunity to see yourself as a person worthy of self-compassion and love, simply because of who you are at the deepest level.

- Please free-write on the following topics:
    - A time when you acted in a generous way
    - A time when you did something thoughtful for another person
    - Ten nice things you have done for others
    - How you have been a good friend or care-taker (either to a person or animal)

- An instance when you were sensitive to another person's needs
- A time when you really cared about doing something the right way
- A time when you went above and beyond what was called for
- A time when you extended yourself to another, even though you didn't need to

- Make a list of ten things you like about yourself
- Make a list of ten things you have done in your life that you are proud of
- What makes you different from other people?
- What risks have you taken?
- What are 5 challenges that you have had to overcome?
- List 3 fears (big or small) that you have faced and overcome
- What is the hardest thing you have ever had to overcome?
- What makes you a survivor?
- How have you made a difference (big or small) in another person's life? List 5 examples.

- Now write a paragraph summarizing your philosophy about what it means to be human. Think about how your philosophy will allow you to connect with a sense of self-worth and self-compassion.

- Based on what you have written above, create a single sentence that you can tell yourself in order to connect with your self-compassion. Having a "mantra" will allow you to easily remind yourself why you have worth – for just being human. So memorize it. And if you'd like, write it out and post it where you can see it every day (for example, on the dashboard of your car or on your bathroom mirror).

Self-Compassion Exercise

Here is a strategy for connecting with your own sense of self-compassion, using the power of your imagination. This is an important exercise because many people have not had the experience of receiving compassion and kindness.

Make sure you can be in a space where you won't be disturbed. Read over these instructions first in order to become familiar with them. Have your journal out where you can access it easily. When you are ready, you can either lay or sit down. The most important thing is that you are comfortable. You can close your eyes during this exercise or keep them open, whichever you prefer.

1. Think about a relationship you have had in the past or have in the present, either with a person or an animal, that is meaningful to you. Now imagine that this person or animal is in need and that you can help it by being kind and compassionate. Take some time to access those feelings.
2. Notice where in your body you have those sensations of kindness and compassion for another. Take as much time as you need to pay attention to where those feelings are residing. When you are ready, place your hands on that spot. Allow yourself

to really **notice** what those sensations feel like with your hands. Perhaps you notice a temperature change. Or a tingling. It's different for each person.

3. Now choose a spot on or in your body where you think it would be natural for you to receive compassion. Follow your intuition in picking this spot. For example, it could be your heart. Or your belly. Or your whole body.

4. Imagine gently directing that energy - and that feeling - toward that location with your hands. Spend some time with your hands on that spot. Notice how it feels when compassion and kindness are moving in **your** direction. Notice how it feels when **you** are the one who is doing that directing to yourself.

5. When you are ready, give yourself permission to allow an image or symbol to coalesce in your mind's eye that reflects these feelings of self-compassion and kindness.

6. Notice its details; its color(s); texture; shape; size.

7. Ask this form if it is OK for you to ask it some questions.

8. Ask it:
    a. How can you assist me?
    b. What can you teach me?
    c. How can I fully experience you?
    d. What message do you have for me?

9. When you are ready, return back to your alert, waking state. Write as much as you can remember in your journal. What have you learned about yourself? How will you integrate what you have learned from this experience into your daily life?

Getting "selfish" about self-care

I have found that people often feel guilty about being nice to themselves because doing so somehow means that they are "selfish". This is an obstacle to self-compassion that it is time to address.

People generally find it easier to show compassion and kindness to another person or animal than to themselves. So I'd like you now to think of something or someone that you have loved unconditionally—a pet, stuffed animal, friend, parent, partner, or child. I'm sure you can do this, since you just did so in the previous exercise. You know that when you love someone or something unconditionally, it means that there are no strings attached. You will always love and want the best for that person or animal no matter what they do to you or someone else. You might disapprove of their actions or be disappointed by something they did, but you still love and care about them. And you especially won't hesitate to attend to that person or animal when you see that they are in need.

So what gets in the way of showing that same compassion to yourself? An answer I typically hear is: "I feel like I am being selfish if I pay attention to myself." But I believe that paying attention to yourself and giving yourself nurturing is not selfish. This is because you need to balance the energy you give out to others with energy that you take in for yourself. If you continually give away your energy, eventually you will end up depleted. That is why it is not selfish to rejuvenate. If you identify as a helper, or are a parent, remember: in order to be of assistance, you need energy!

If other people do not respect your need to replenish your energy, they are giving you clear feedback about their lack of concern for your well-being. This is why **boundaries** are so important. Boundaries are standards and limits a person sets in order to let others know what behavior is acceptable or unacceptable. By being clear to others about your needs, you are teaching people how to treat you. In that way, your boundaries act as your protection. You will be able to take care of yourself by setting and maintaining boundaries, and making sure that other people respect them.

If you are not willing to set and maintain boundaries, then what is it that you are afraid of?

Journal questions

- How easy is it for you to be "selfish"?
- If you are "selfish," what are you afraid will happen?
- Why is OK to sacrifice your own needs for taking care of others?
- What is difficult about saying "no" when somebody asks you to do something for them?
- Why is it OK to give but not to receive?
- What could you tell yourself that would make it easier for you to attend to your own needs?
- What could you tell yourself that would make it easier for you to say "no" to somebody (if doing so is in your best interests)? What message could you tell yourself that would release you from feeling guilty afterwards?

- How easy is it for you to tell yourself, "I am worth it"?
- Do you feel guilty when you do something nice for yourself? Why? What are you telling yourself?
- What could you say to challenge that part of you that makes you feel guilty about doing nice things for yourself?
- When somebody gives you a complement, how do you respond?
    - Is it easy for you to accept it?
    - If it is difficult, what gets in the way?
    - What could you tell yourself that would make it easier for you to accept a compliment?

Now let's get a sense of how you are doing in terms of self-care:

- How do you keep yourself deprived?
- How do you currently show yourself affection? How have you done so in the past?
- How do you currently show yourself appreciation? How have you done so in the past?
- What do currently you do for fun? What have you done in the past?
- What do you currently do for relaxation? What are some other things that you could do for relaxation that you haven't yet tried?
- What currently gives you pleasure? What have you done in the past that has given you pleasure?

There are many ways to nurture yourself. Here are some journal prompts to get you started. The answers will provide you with plenty of ideas you can use to bring self-care into your life.

- What are some people, places and things that bring a smile to your face?
- List 20 things that you have enjoyed doing in the past
- List 20 things you currently enjoy doing
- List 20 ways to nourish yourself
- Make a list of 100 things that you love (there is no need to fill this in during one sitting; keep this as an open list and add to it as things occur to you. Nothing is too small or trivial!)

- Finally, complete this sentence: **If I had enough time, I would:**

Based on what you've written above, please answer the following questions:

- What is something you can do to spiritually nourish yourself today?
- What is the smallest thing you can do today to make yourself feel good?
- What are three things you can commit to doing this week to nurture yourself?
- What is something you could do in the next month to "recharge your batteries"?
- What or who would you like to add to your life?
- What or who would you like to drop from your life?

- Create a list of the rules you would like to live your life by that will serve your best interests
- Make a list of the top ten things you will no longer be doing or accepting in your life
- Now create a self-compassion mantra. What can you tell yourself in order to nourish and sustain your feelings of care and kindness towards yourself?

Hopefully, you now have a bunch of ideas you can use to help you decide how to nurture yourself. Think about how you might incorporate some of those ideas into your life on a daily basis. Create an action plan – and see how easy or difficult it is to follow through. **The key is to start small, since that will create a sense of consistency and success.** Then, as you are able, keep adding!

Remember that food also plays a role in self-nurturance. Every time you make a decision about what to eat – and how to eat it – you have the opportunity to present a gift to your body and your soul.

***

Here is a challenge for you. Each day for a week, see if you can:

- Notice 5 things that go right
- Pick one way in which to nurture yourself – and do it
- Pick one way to comfort yourself – and do it
- Make a promise to yourself – and keep it
- Do something nice for yourself
- Do something nice for another person or animal

Please journal on the following:

As you did (or considered doing) each of the above tasks, what thoughts and feelings came up for you? If you were able to complete the tasks, what messages were you telling yourself? If you were unable to complete a task, what was blocking you?

Feeling compassion and gratitude for your body

Self-compassion also includes thinking about how your physical body has served you. Take some time to think about what a miracle your body is. It has been working hard for you since before you were even born!

Consider these facts:

- Each day a mature body produces three hundred billion cells in order to replenish and maintain the body's total of seventy-five trillion cells.
- Although your heart weighs less than a pound, it pumps three thousand gallons of blood through you each and every day.
- You are born with about 300 bones but by the time you're an adult you're left with about 200, due to bones fusing together. Your skeleton gives structure to your body, and protects your vital organs.
- Your hand has incredible capabilities, extending and flexing millions of times over a lifetime.
- The marrow of your bones manufacture 2.5 million red blood cells each second, as it works to renew a supply of twenty-five trillion red blood cells.

- Your body has 650 muscles. When you take a step you use two hundred of them (not only in your foot and leg, but also using those in your back and abdomen for balance).
- Every moment of every day your lungs are working. They take in fresh air and expel waste gases in order to bring in the oxygen that is necessary for every cell in your body. At rest you breathe about 12-15 times a minute. That's at least 17,000 breaths in just a single day!
- Your body is continually producing new cells to replace dying cells and to repair damaged ones. When something happens that negatively impacts the integrity of your body (from a sunburn to a small cut to a broken bone), all kinds of healing processes spring into action.
- Then there is your liver. It has over 500 vital processes. In addition, it processes all nutrients absorbed by the intestines and neutralizes toxins. Amazingly, it will still function if up to 80 percent of it is destroyed or cut away, and can rebuild itself in just a few months to its original size!

As you can see, the human body is truly amazing. Unfortunately, it is easy to take our bodies for granted. It often is not until we become ill or lose the functioning of a particular body part that we begin to appreciate our physical selves.

Your body exists to serve you, as best it can. What and how you eat directly affects its ability to support you.

Body appreciation exercise

Set aside at least an hour when you can be alone. Find a full-length mirror and stand in front of it. You can either be naked or clothed. As you look at your reflection, consider the miracles of your body. It is designed to serve you from the moment you are conceived until the day you die.

As you remain standing in front of a mirror, spend some time considering each part of your body.

1. Recall how it has served and/or continues to serve you
2. Thank it
3. Tell it that you love it
4. Notice the thoughts and feeling that come up as you do this exercise

Now laying or sitting down, close your eyes and simply put your hands on an area of your body that you do not like.

- What thoughts or feelings come up for you?
- Express in words how you feel to this body part.
- Then ask it what it needs from you
- Then consider: Can you provide what it needs? What might get in the way? How could you best address that obstacle?

Do this exercise for each of the body parts that you don't like or don't feel connected to. When you are done, spend some time writing in your journal about what you experienced and how it made you feel.

Journal prompts:

- How has your body taken care of you in the past?

- How does your body currently take care of you?

- What can you do to say "Thank you" to your body?

- What are some different ways you could acknowledge what your body does for you every day?

- How can you recognize and honor what your body has done for you in the past?

- How can you use food and eating to honor your body?

Developing compassion for your digestive system

Now I would like to focus on one specific aspect of your internal world: the digestive system. Most of us are divorced from this process – since we can't see inside ourselves, it is easy to ignore what goes on there. But perhaps if we had an idea of what happens to food once we eat it, and how hard our bodies work every minute of every day to digest and use what we eat, we might be able to show our physical selves more kindness.

Our digestive system is a beautifully interconnected network that runs itself. From the time we are born until the day we die, we are continually creating and recreating our bodies through the food we eat. Every moment throughout our lives, our digestive system is working to turn the food we eat into particles that our cells can use for energy, growth, maintenance, and repair.

(If you are unfamiliar with the shapes, sizes and locations of particular organs, your assignment is to do some research on the internet. Take some time to search for a diagram of the digestive system that you can use as a reference.)

After taking food into your mouth, chewing begins the digestive process by breaking it down. It is there that one of your most important body fluids comes into play – saliva, produced by the salivary glands. Mostly water, your saliva contains digestive enzymes that initiate the digestion of starches. The liquid nature of saliva allows the bolus (the soft mass of chewed food) to go down the esophagus more easily. In addition, saliva provides an important bath for your mouth! It not only contains minerals that support healthy teeth, but also ensures that your mouth has a proper PH (acid/alkaline) balance.

Next, the food moves down a narrow tube called the esophagus into your stomach. Located under the heart, the stomach turns food into chyme, which is a soupy liquid. Hydorchloric acid, which is produced by cells in the stomach lining, begins to dismantle the proteins in food. It also kills unfriendly microbes in what you've eaten. This acid is strong, but your stomach is protected by a thick coating of mucus. Although most foods pass through the stomach without being fully assimilated into your body, alcohol, water, and some salts enter the bloodstream directly from the stomach.

From the stomach, food enters your small intestine, which if stretched out to its full length, would measure on average 15 to 20 feet. This is where food is digested and absorbed into the blood stream. The intestinal lining also blocks the absorption of particles that are considered "foreign substances," which are then earmarked for elimination by the body.

Your pancreas has two main roles. First, it helps to neutralize the acidity of the chyme so that it does not burn the tissues of the intestines. Second, it creates and secretes enzymes that digest fats, carbohydrates and protein, which then allow them to be absorbed into the bloodstream.

The liver plays a crucial role in digestion and typically works overtime. It creates bile which emulsifies fats for digestion; makes and breaks down many hormones, including cholesterol, estrogen, and testosterone; regulates blood sugar levels; and processes all of the food – and other materials – which enter your blood stream. The liver acts on nutrients in order to make them usable to your body's cells.

The gall bladder, which lies just below the liver, stores and concentrates the bile which is produced by the liver. Bile breaks down fats, cholesterol, and fat-soluble vitamins into particles that are then easier for digestion.

After all the nutrients have been absorbed, water, fiber and bacteria pass into the large intestine (or colon). This is short, only 3 – 5 feet long. It absorbs water and also forms stool. Trillions of bacteria live in the colon. Its friendly bacteria help your body fight illness.

After the stool is well-formed, it gets pushed down into the descending colon and then into the rectum. It remains there until there is enough of it for a bowel movement.

So there you go – the food you eat takes quite a journey through your body, doesn't it! A *lot* is going on every minute of every day inside of you. I believe that if you consider what actually happens to food once you eat it, your relationship with it might change. And perhaps if you understand all of the hard work your body is doing every moment of every day, you would be more inclined to treat it with compassion. Your body is truly doing its best to serve you!

Exercise

Please search out a picture of your digestive system, which you can easily access one online. Make sure you find one that resonates with you. I would like you to take several moments to simply look at this picture with gentle, soft eyes. Think of this exercise as a meditation in which you connect with your curiosity - imagine that you are seeing this aspect of your body for the first time.

Notice where particular organs are located in your body and how large or small each one is. Study each of their shapes and positions. I would like you to get a sense of what is going on inside of you. Lift up your shirt a little bit and notice the flesh of your abdomen. Because you now know what lies beneath it, spend some time going between the diagram and your belly. See if you can connect with the fact that there is a whole world inside of you dedicated to your well-being that is invisible to your eyes. Do any of your observations surprise you? What are you learning about the inside of your body?

When you have finished this exercise, please answer the following two journal questions:

- If your digestive system could communicate, what message would it give you?
- How might your knowledge of your digestive system affect what and how you eat?

Honoring your needs

What are needs and how are they connected to self-compassion? I believe that an important way to show yourself kindness is by acknowledging that your needs are valid and deserve to be met.

Tellingly, the word "need" comes from the West Saxon (Old English) noun *nied*, meaning "necessity, compulsion, duty." It is also related to the Czech *nyti* which means "to languish." A need, whether physical or emotional, is something that is necessary for a person's well-being. When a need is fulfilled, we feel healthy and satisfied. Unfulfilled needs leave us with ill-health, frustration and resentment.

As humans, we all share the physical needs of oxygen, water, and food. Different emotional needs, however, will resonate either more strongly or weakly with us because each person is unique. But in varying degrees, most of us have a need to feel:

- Safe and Secure

- Connected with others

- Acknowledged

- A sense of control

- Loved and accepted

- That there is meaning in our life

Our current behaviors, thoughts, and feelings are often generated in response to needs that did not get addressed when we were children. Because they were not filled, these needs continue to haunt us throughout life and into adulthood.

Journal exercises

- What did you need as a child from your parents/caregivers that you did not receive? Create a fantasy in which you received the perfect nurturing from your parents. What would you have been given? What would you have heard your parents say to you?

- Can you accept having needs without feeling selfish? If not, what is it that you are telling yourself that prevents you? From whom did you learn those messages?

- Please ask yourself the following questions, and free write the answers:

  - What do I want for myself?

- What are 10 important things for me to do?
- What do I need to have?
- What do I need to know?
- What do I need to do?
- What do I hunger for?
- What makes me feel loved?
- What makes life feel magical?
- What is unlived in my life that is required for my life to be more complete and whole?

Number a page from 1-30. Now, off the top of your head, list as many of your needs as you can. Some examples might be: Solitude; having close friendships; quality time with your children; a fulfilling job; being really listened to by your partner; the opportunity to be creative.

If you can't fill in all 30 slots in one sitting, then simply keep the list open and add to it over the course of a week. When you have finished, please answer the following questions:

- How many of your needs are currently being met?
- For each need that is not being met or is not being sufficiently met, please answer:
  - What emotion(s) do you feel when you think about this need not being met?
  - What thoughts come to mind?
  - What behavior(s) do you engage in due to the need not being met?
  - What is the cost to you of this need not being met?
  - What change(s) would occur in your life if the need were met?

- What has to happen for the need to be met?
- How can you strengthen your commitment to fulfilling that need?

Now let's address the needs of your physical body.

First, in your journal, you will create a dialogue. Please use two differently colored pens for this exercise, one for you, the other for your body. Begin by asking your body: "What do you need from me?" Then, from the perspective of your body, according to your best guess, answer that question. Your second question for your body is: "How can I best serve you?" Again, imagine you are your body, and do your best to answer the question. The feedback you get from these two questions is important for you to know.

Next, please write down each of these statements:

1. My body deserves to be nourished
2. My body deserves to be treated with respect
3. My body deserves to wear comfortable clothing and shoes
4. My body deserves affectionate touch
5. My body deserves to move through the world with ease

What thoughts and feelings come up for you as you write and consider each of these statements? What, if anything, prevents your body from having these needs met? What can you begin to do (on a daily/weekly/monthly basis) to begin to honor the various needs of your body?

Forgiving Yourself

I did then what I knew how to do. Now that I know better, I do better.
    Maya Angelou

Another key component to developing self-compassion is the ability to forgive oneself. It is my experience that people often treat themselves poorly because they believe they have to punish themselves for something they did wrong in the past.

Forgiveness means recognizing that there are things that occurred in the past for which there is no way to go back and change. Forgiveness entails releasing the desire that things had happened differently. This does not necessarily mean accepting what has happened. Rather, it means making peace with the fact that something has happened, and releasing anger, shame and guilt. Until we reach a point where we are ready to forgive, our bitterness and disappointment reside in us as toxic substances, and act as barriers to self-compassion. As Nelson Mandela pointed out, "Resentment is like drinking poison and then hoping it will kill your enemies."

Indeed, some people use food and eating as a means to punish themselves. Because they believe that they deserve to be punished, it is easier for them to treat their bodies poorly.

Journal exercise:

Look back over your life and:

- make a list of things that you regret doing
- make a list of things that you regret not doing
- make a list of things you did that you are angry at yourself about
- make a list of things about which you are ashamed at yourself

For each entry on your lists, ask yourself:

- At that time, what need was I trying to meet?
- What was I thinking to myself?
- What feeling or emotion was I experiencing?

The next step is to accept what happened and to forgive yourself. You can do this by telling yourself:

I was doing the best I could have been doing in that moment. If I could have done something differently, I would have. Therefore, I accept myself without judgment. I was trying to get my needs met in the only way I knew how at that time. I wish it would not have happened but it did. And so I forgive myself. I am willing to move on. I am ready to move forward in my life.

Finally, and perhaps most importantly, for each item on your lists, please fill in the following:

"I am proud of myself because..."

It is also vital to be able to forgive yourself in the present. You have to continually remind yourself that you are doing the best you can in this moment. Always keep in mind the Maya Angelou quote from above: If you could be doing something differently, you would - so give yourself a break!

Cultivating gratitude

Let us rise up and be thankful, for if we didn't learn a lot today, at least we learned a little, and if we didn't learn a little, at least we didn't get sick, and if we got sick, at least we didn't die. So let us all be thankful.

the Buddha

Gratitude is connected to a sense of appreciation, recognition, and love for people, places, and things in your life. Gratitude is also a very important factor in creating self-kindness. This is because in order to have self-compassion, you have to be able to *appreciate* who you are and why you are the way you are. By focusing on what you are thankful for, you will shift your attention in a positive direction. As you begin to pay attention to what you appreciate about your life and who you are as a person, it will become easier for you to show yourself compassion. In turn, it will become easier for you to nourish your body in a positive way with food.

Journal exercises:

- What is currently going right for you in your life?

- How can you honor what is going right in your life?

- Make a list of 20 things you are grateful for.

- What are the blessings in your life?

- Currently in your life:

    - What are you happy about?

    - What are you excited about?

    - What are you proud of?

    - What are you *most* grateful for?

    - What are you enjoying?

    - What are you committed to?

    - Who do you love?

    - Who loves you?

A powerful way to connect with gratitude is the next exercise, which was developed by Tony Robbins. Each evening before bed, meditate on or journal about the following three questions. They will provide you with a powerful new perspective that will activate your sense of gratitude.

1. What have I given today?
2. What did I receive today?
3. What did I learn today?

Another effective tool for developing a sense of appreciation and self-compassion is **The Gratitude Journal**.

Each day, at a specific time, in a special journal dedicated solely to this task, center yourself, and then list three things you are thankful for. Of course, if you are feeling inspired, you can certainly list more than three. But your benchmark of success with this ritual is three, since that is within the realm of possibility for everyone, no matter how busy. Please write as much or as little with each entry as you choose. If you do have the time, though, I believe that writing in more detail about each entry can deepen your sense of gratitude more than a simple list will.

I also feel that if you can avoid hurrying through this ritual, you will reap greater benefits. Ideally, as you finish writing each item on your list, you will take some time to savor the gift you have been presented with. Notice how it feels to relish each blessing in your life (no matter how big or small). Try to connect with both an emotional and physical sense of how deep your gratitude runs for each item.

I would like to emphasize that you don't have to think too hard about what to be grateful for. You can list major events in your life if you'd like. Perhaps you're grateful for a raise at work. Or that you finished a marathon. But don't be afraid to write about the simple or mundane things that you generally take for granted, such as being able to take a deep breath without pain. Or the smell of fresh flowers. Or a baby's smile. At the same time, perhaps you might want to remind yourself that you have a roof over your head. Or running water. Or that you woke up this morning.

As far as what you actually write, simply follow your intuition. There is no right or wrong way to keep a Gratitude Journal. But to give you a sense of how to start, you could simply use these sentence stems:

"Today I am grateful for..."

"Today I am grateful that..."

The beautiful thing about the ritual of the Gratitude Journal is that with each passing day, you will begin to notice the abundance in your life, rather than the lack. In addition, if you start to consider how your life would be without those people or things you are thankful for, your sense of gratitude and well-being will only deepen. And in turn, so will your feelings of compassion, kindness and understanding for yourself.

***

No discussion about gratitude would be complete without including the suggestion of offering thanks before a meal. Most of us are familiar with "saying grace," which comes from the Latin expression "*gratiarum actio*," meaning "an act of thanks." We often think about this is in a religious context, since in the United States saying grace before a meal is associated with Christianity. However, offering a blessing before eating is found universally in all cultures. Certainly, for some people, thanking their Higher Power for its life-giving force or the earth for its bounty is an important devotional ritual. Yet in our fast-paced, hurried and harried world, it is very easy to bypass saying grace, and just jump right into eating.

That is why I would like you to consider saying grace for at least one meal each day. Doing so is a simple way to connect with gratitude and appreciation.

You can begin by thanking God or your Higher Power or Mother Earth. But I also believe it can be a profound experience to spend time before each meal thinking about all of the people whose efforts have led to the food that is sitting on your plate: The farmers, the harvesters, the people who packaged the food, those who transported it, the clerks at the store who shelved it, the person who went out and bought it, and then whoever cooked it. Plus, if you are eating part of an animal, it is important to recognize that it gave its life for your nourishment. Thus does each integral part of a long chain deserve your thanks.

Introducing the tradition of saying grace into your life is powerful for several reasons. It forces you to slow down, pay attention, and consider your meal. And as I mentioned earlier in the book, eating is the most intimate thing you can do, as the food you consume actually becomes part of your body. That is why the act of saying grace transforms what could be a mundane, rushed or thoughtless act into the sacred, deliberate ritual it truly is.

There is no right or wrong way to say grace. It can be done in silence, spoken, sung – and even signed. I know one family whose members, all together as a group, simply repeat "Thank you" out loud seven or eight times before each meal. Then there are the multitudes of blessings from religious and cultural traditions, ranging from the simple "Bless this food," to lengthy prayers.

The bottom line is this: If you choose to begin to say grace before each meal, think about the words that would resonate with you. Remember, this isn't about going through the motions. Rather, it is about communicating a heart-felt sense of gratitude for the opportunity (and privilege) to eat a meal. Thus, the best mealtime prayers will flow spontaneously as you follow your intuition and trust your soul to provide the right words for you.

***

Checking In:

- **What changes have you noticed in your life since beginning this program?**
- **What are some things you have learned about yourself?**
- **How is your sense of gratitude for others impacting how you appreciate yourself?**
- **How is your self-appreciation influencing how you treat other people?**
- **Based on the work you have done in this chapter, how easy is it for you to believe that simply because you are alive, you are a worthwhile human being?**
- **What are you noticing about your relationship with food?**
- **What are some ways you can use food and eating to treat yourself with compassion and kindness?**

***

The next three chapters will show you how to control your thoughts and beliefs so that they don't get in the way of your efforts to change. Therefore, they form an important component of *The Buddha Diet*. Each skill that you learn will allow you to confidently handle the mental obstacles that get in the way of treating yourself with kindness and compassion. It is so important to pay attention to your mental state because that is what typically causes a person to self-sabotage.

The negative beliefs we have about ourselves and the world around us, as well as the critical things we tell ourselves, will quickly derail us if we let them. When negative thoughts gain the upper hand, they create negative emotions, which make it all too easy to treat our bodies poorly and eat foods we know aren't good for us. I have seen again and again how a person's belief system, negative thinking, and inner critic can short-circuit a healthy relationship with food and eating.

In addition, it is helpful to understand how your thoughts influence your emotions, which in turn determine how you digest and assimilate food into your body. That is why the psychological focus of the next three chapters is an integral part of this program.

Consider the following description of the interplay between psychology and physiology:

In order to take advantage of nutrients, your body has to provide the means to carefully break them down into much smaller molecules that can be imported into blood. But the digestive tract is particularly sensitive to stress and strong emotions. This is because digestion is controlled by what is known as the enteric nervous system, a subdivision of the autonomic nervous system (which regulates things such as heart rate, respiration, and sexual arousal). This network is made up of hundreds of millions of nerves that communicate with the central nervous system. These nerves are sensitive to the hormones produced by stress.

When stress activates the "flight or fight" response in your central nervous system, energy moves to physiological functions necessary for survival in the moment. This affects the digestive process in a number of significant ways: Blood used for digestion gets moved to other areas of the body. Muscular contractions necessary for digestion become sharper and less rhythmic. Digestive secretions are thrown out of balance. The esophagus can go into spasms. The acid in the stomach increases, which can cause indigestion. In addition, the stomach becomes unable to process food effectively. The colon can then become inflamed, leading to either diarrhea or constipation.

Now let's move to the top of the body. The human brain is electrical in nature. It communicates its messages to specific sites in the body by sending electrochemical impulses via the central nervous system. So thoughts are actually pulses of energy. And because they are energetic waves that radiate outward, they affect every single cell in our bodies. This highlights the mind-body connection, since our bodies react to our thoughts. Think of a polygraph machine. What and how we think can change our body temperature, blood pressure, heart rate, muscle tension, and breathing rate.

Compounding this is the fact that our brain can have a hard time differentiating between reality and imagination. For example, if I ask you to imagine sucking on a slice of a yellow, juicy lemon, chances are you will begin to salivate. So even though the lemon is physically absent, your memory of its sour taste is enough to initiate a physiological response. This is why worrying about the future or dwelling in the past can be so physically debilitating.

Not only that, research has also found that the kinds of thinking we do will release certain chemicals into our blood stream. Positive thinking and feelings such as joy and pleasure release chemicals like serotonin and endorphins, which in turn bolster a good mood. Negative thoughts release chemicals like cortisol, too much of which stresses our adrenal glands.

The bottom line is that your mental and emotional states before, during, and after a meal have a significant impact on how you digest that meal and assimilate the nutrients of the food you have just eaten. That is why it is so important for you to have the ability to address a negative belief system, irrational thoughts, and your inner critic.

Chapter 7

Skill #4: Overcoming Maladaptive Beliefs

We don't see things as they are, we see them as we are.

Anais Nin

I asked myself, 'What is the myth you are living?' and found that I did not know. So...I took it upon myself to get to know 'my' myth and regarded this as the task of tasks...I simply had to know what unconscious or preconscious myth was forming me.

Carl Jung

Most of us have become so accustomed to acting out our internal version of ourselves that we are no longer aware that just because we believe something doesn't make it true. Just because we've been living according to particular beliefs for twenty or fifty years does not mean they have one shred of validity...

Geneen Roth

A belief system is a set of ideas that develops during childhood or adolescence. These ideas consist of important beliefs and feelings about oneself and the environment. Like tinted glasses, a person views the world through his or her belief system. Some belief systems are liberating and empowering. Others are maladaptive; that is, they are limiting and destructive.

Of course, when it comes to food, a person's belief system is highly influential. This is because it affects the why, when, how and what of eating.

Generally, a person carries his or her belief system into adulthood. This is because these ideas about life are self-perpetuating, and are very resistant to change. Like a person who has only a hammer, every situation in life (and throughout one's life) comes to look just like a nail...For instance, a child who develops the idea that she is incompetent will rarely challenge this belief, even as an adult. She will interpret her experiences in life as supporting her belief system. And at the same time, because her belief system is deeply embedded in her psyche, she will ignore or discount those experiences which challenge it.

Our experience quite literally is defined by our assumptions about life...We make stories about the world and to a large degree live out their plots. What our lives are like depends to a great extent on the script we consciously, or more likely, unconsciously, have adopted.

Carol Pearson

It is vital that you seek to understand the belief system that governs your life. You can do so by examining the values, assumptions, ideals and ideologies which influence (and constrain) the way you think, feel and act. Once you have gained insight into how you process reality, you can then decide if it is necessary to reprogram yourself with a new belief system that serves your best interests. In particular, it will be necessary for you to have a belief system that allows you to have a healthy, positive relationship with food and eating. The key to unlocking a negative belief system is understanding that *you were not born with it.* It is not your fate. It can be changed.

One discovers that destiny can be directed, that one does not have to remain in bondage to the first imprint made on childhood sensibilities. Once the deforming mirror has been smashed, there is a possibility of wholeness. There is a possibility of joy.

Anais Nin

Therefore, a very important question to ask yourself is:

Where did my basic assumptions and ideas about myself and the world around me originate?

Often you learned these assumptions and ideas from the same people and places that provided you with your original value system:

- Societal norms
- Family
- The media
- Community (peers; friends; religious institutions; teachers)
- Feedback from our own experiences

So consider this: What you consider "reality" might simply be a collection of ideas, perceptions, assumptions, expectations, and opinions that you have come to accept about you and the world around you. These belief systems are usually not entirely accurate. In fact, they are often far from the truth.

Remember, your basic assumptions frame the world you live in and provide the meaning you find in it. But most people are not conscious of their assumptions. This misperception may prevent you from seeing things as they really are. That is, instead of spontaneously *responding* to something appropriately, you might automatically *react* to it the way you always have. In that sense, your beliefs do not allow you to engage with reality on a moment by moment basis, since you are trapped in the past.

Below are some examples of negative belief systems. Notice if any sound familiar to you.

- The world is a dangerous place.
- People can't be trusted.
- Women shouldn't work.
- Men aren't dependable.
- Life isn't fair.
- I am a bad person.
- I will never fit in.
- I am incapable of being independent.
- I am weak.
- I need other people to validate me.
- I should be able to do whatever I want.
- It's always my fault.
- It's never my fault.
- My needs don't matter.
- It is OK for me to deprive myself.
- It's best to take care of others.
- My worth is based on other people's opinions of me.
- Life is hard.
- It's not good to show emotions.
- I always should be perfect.
- It's not good to make mistakes.
- Success is being materially wealthy.

Some core beliefs about food and eating:

- Vegetables are boring.
- Cooking is difficult.
- I should never waste food.
- It's not dinner without dessert.
- Only thin people are attractive.

- Overweight people are undisciplined.
- Foods that are "good for you" aren't tasty.
- I simply can't control how much I eat.

The following journal questions will assist you in developing a sense of your core beliefs and how they developed.

- What is "The Story" of your life?
    - First, list out each year of your life, beginning with the year you were born. Then go back and fill in as much as you can remember about what you experienced during that year.
    - Next, I would like you to spend some time writing your autobiography in narrative form, either in first or third person. (it can be as long as you'd like)
    - Now I would like you to summarize your life in:
        - a single page
        - a single paragraph
        - two sentences
        - a single sentence
        - choose a single word from that last sentence to characterize the entirety of your life
- When you were growing up, what kinds of things did you tell yourself about the world and your place in it?
- As you look back over your life, what major themes do you notice?

- Currently, what do you tell yourself about the world and your place in it?
- Based on what you've written above, what are some new themes you would like to manifest in your life as you move forward into the future?

Think back to a negative defining moment you have had in your life. This is something that happened to you or something somebody said to you that has stuck with you and influenced how you feel about yourself and/or the world. In your journal, please answer the following questions:

- What happened?
- What did you learn about life?
- What did you learn about yourself?
- In believing that this is true, how do you suffer?
- If you were able to release this belief, how would your life change?
- Just for a moment, imagine this belief as something you can lay to the side. You can always pick it back up, but just for a moment, imagine laying it down. Notice how you feel.

Belief Exercise

This next exercise is extensive, but will allow you to do a full inventory of your beliefs so that you can decide what to do about them. Having a clear sense of your belief system and whether it serves you or not will allow you avoid self-sabotage as you change your relationship with food and eating.

This is not an exercise to be rushed through, so be sure to allow yourself enough time to complete it, either in one or multiple sessions.

At the top of a journal page write the heading, **"This I believe:"** Underneath, write the numbers one through twelve. Now take some time to become centered and clear your mind. I would like you to try your best to fill in all ten spaces with what you believe about the world, people in general, and yourself, using the sentence stem: **I believe that**:

As you write down each belief, see if you can remember how you came to that conclusion about life, and write that down as well under each belief.

When you have finally finished writing, you will have a collection of beliefs that govern your life, as well as a sense of their origins.

Now, using a separate page in your journal, I would like you to answer the following questions for each one:

1. What has this belief helped me to accomplish?
2. What has this belief helped me to avoid?
3. What does this belief allow me to do?
4. What does this belief allow me to have?

5. What does this belief allow me to be?
6. What are the advantages of this belief?
7. How do I use this belief against others?
8. What has this belief gotten me into?
9. What has this belief gotten me out of?
10. What has this belief solved?
11. What is the value of this belief?
12. What is the importance of this belief?
13. When would this belief be a good idea?
14. When would this belief not be a good idea?

Finally: Each of your rules and beliefs has consequences. For each one, please answer the following two questions.

1. What happens when I have this belief?
2. What would happen if I didn't have this belief?

Now go back and take an inventory of your beliefs. Get a sense of which ones expand the possibilities in your life and give you energy. Notice the ones which limit you and drain your energy.

To avoid self-sabotage as you make changes in your life, it is necessary for you to understand the role your beliefs have played in determining your perspective on life. You must remind yourself that you do not have to be a slave to your beliefs – they are not set in stone.

So having lived your life with a particular belief system – and knowing how it has affected you – what would you change about it? Which beliefs would you like to keep? Which would you like to release? And what might be some new empowering beliefs about the world that you could add?

This is your chance to create a supportive belief framework as you transform your relationship with food and eating. Some examples of beliefs that will make your journey easier:

- I deserve to be loved.
- I am a worthwhile human being.
- I am unique.
- I have faith in myself.
- I can trust my body.
- It is OK to make mistakes.
- It is OK to be nice to myself.
- I am open to new experiences.
- I am stronger than I realize.
- I won't let perfect get in the way of good enough.
- It is OK to take risks.
- I don't have to be perfect.
- I am strong enough to love another person.
- It is OK for me to receive love and support.
- It is important for me to show my emotions.
- I am willing to make mistakes as long as I learn from them.
- I don't need approval from other people.
- I am comfortable trusting my intuition.
- People can change.
- The world is a supportive, giving place.
- Success is being content with what I already have.

Journal Exercise

Make a list of the beliefs that you would like to consciously bring into your life. These are beliefs that support you, empower you, and allow you to be kind to yourself. Your belief system should *not* lead to feelings of guilt, shame, or unworthiness. If you would like, you can also create a collage or make some other artwork that revolves around your new world view.

It might take time for your new belief system to truly sink in because you have been living with your old one for so many years. Please be patient and take the time to remind yourself *why* you have decided to shift your core beliefs. An easy way to do that is by reviewing the exercises you did in this chapter. As you begin to feel better and see how your relationship with food and eating is shifting, your new perspective will reinforce itself.

Chapter 8

Skill #5: Neutralizing Negative Self-Talk

The mind is everything. What you think, you become.

    the Buddha

To enjoy good health, to bring true happiness to one's family, to bring peace to all, one must first discipline and control one's own mind.

    the Buddha

Another road-block that gets in the way of positive change is **negative thinking**. As you journey toward creating a positive relationship with food and eating, the things you tell yourself have the potential to either support you or derail you. This chapter is focused on making sure you are able to stay on track.

Everyone has voices in their heads – that's just part of being human. It is natural to carry on a conversation with ourselves in our minds, and most of us do it all the time.

However, our mental chatter sometimes communicates things that make us feel badly about ourselves or our lives. These negative thoughts lead to feelings such as depression, anxiety, and low self-esteem. We often take our distressing inner monologue seriously because it sounds rational and accurate.

Our negative thinking prevents us from making positive changes in our lives because it scares us and reaffirms the negative views we have of the world. As you will learn, however, those negative thoughts are flawed, and by believing them, you buy into the maladaptive core beliefs we discussed in the last chapter.

The skill you will learn in this chapter is how to recognize and address those negative thoughts (also known as "cognitive distortions"), so that they do not control your life or limit your choices. The good news is that because your negative thinking is learned, you can un-learn it.

At this point, you might be wondering what the differences are between your core negative belief system and your negative thinking. Think of your belief system as the foundation of your house. It is the base that supports and gives shape to the entirety of the home itself. Depending on how that foundation was constructed, your house will have a particular structure. Your negative thinking is represented by specific rooms in your house. Just as a home has many kinds of rooms, from small to large, so too do you have many different types of negative thoughts (which I will describe in more detail below).

So your core belief system is a general way of looking at the world, while your negative thinking consists of particular thoughts that are triggered when specific things happen to you.

For example, let's say that one of your core negative beliefs is "I am a failure," because a parent continually told you that "You can't do anything right." Your negative self-talk will support that belief. When you do poorly on a test you tell yourself, "See, I knew that was going to happen, I'm just not a good student." Or you'll decide not to try out for the softball team, telling yourself, "There's no way I could be good at that." Or when your supervisor at work gives you negative feedback (even if done in a constructive way) you become depressed and think to yourself, "This job is too much for me – I should never have taken it. I'm in over my head. I'll never get the hang of it. I am sure they are going to fire me."

How to discover your "irrational thoughts"

In psychology, we often refer to negative thoughts as "irrational" because they have no basis in objective reality. For example, you may tell yourself, "I don't want to go to that party because I know I'll have a bad time." This thought certainly appears real to you and generates feelings of shame and sadness. But consider this – there is no way to predict the future, which is exactly what you are doing. All negative thinking can be debunked once you challenge its logic. That is why we would call that thought about not wanting to go to the party "irrational."

In order to address your negative beliefs, you must first figure out what your inner monologue actually consists of. The easiest way to do this is by paying attention to the negative messages that you tell yourself as you go through the day. This is when your mindfulness skills will really pay off. Once you are able to recognize those thoughts for what they really are, then you can begin to challenge them. And by neutralizing your negative thinking, you will discover that you have the ability to avoid many of the negative emotions you are used to having. You will also experience a sense of openness and possibility, since you will be able to avoid the constraints your negative thinking imposes on you.

In the next section I will provide a list of the most common cognitive distortions. I would like you to become familiar with this list. Doing so will help you become aware of the patterns of your own negative thinking. You will also see that you are not crazy – everyone has negative thoughts that fall into one or more of these categories. You are not alone!

Examples of Common Cognitive Distortions

Psychologists have discovered that negative thoughts can be grouped into categories based on particular characteristics. As you notice what you tell yourself each day, you can use the list below to "label" your thinking. You will discover that your thoughts will most likely fall into at least one of the following categories. Once you recognize that your thought is "irrational" and not a true reflection of reality, you will see it for what it is, and thereby diminish its power over you.

Each category has a specific example of irrational thinking in action. I have also included a "more helpful response" that will help you to see alternative ways of responding to an event. I worded these "responses" in such a way as to give you an idea of what you might tell or ask yourself in those situations.

- **<u>All or Nothing Thinking</u>**

  You use rigid categories that lead to either/or conclusions; there is no in-between. You think in absolutes such as "always," and "never," which means that you don't believe in exceptions.
  Example: You go on a diet and then sneak a "forbidden food." This makes you feel depressed because you believe you've just ruined the entire diet.
  - **More helpful response:** "Things aren't either totally white or totally black – there are shades of grey. Where is this on the spectrum? Is it *really* true that I've failed at this diet? How can I learn from my mistake and move on?"

- **<u>Over Generalizing</u>**

  You draw the conclusion that a single negative event is actually a never-ending pattern. Even though the case might be isolated, you still believe that it applies to every instance.
  Example: You decide to try a new diet but then give up after several weeks. This leads you to berate yourself: "I can *never* stick with anything!"

○ **More helpful response:** "Is it true that things are **always** or **never** a certain way? Where are the exceptions? Am I exaggerating?"

- ## Mental Filtering

  You focus on a single negative detail about a situation or person, and ignore neutral or positive things.
  Example: You go out for an anniversary meal with your partner. The meal itself is delicious – until desert, which is underwhelming. On the way home, all you do is complain about how disappointing the dinner was.
     ○ **More helpful response:** "Am I only noticing the bad stuff? Am I filtering out the positives? What is a more realistic assessment?"

- ## Disqualifying the Positive

  You reject positive experiences, believing that "they don't count". You maintain a negative view in spite of any evidence that might be contradictory.
  Example: You spend a lot of time cooking and people are always asking you for recipes. But you tell yourself that your food is nothing special, and are skeptical of those who praise it.
     ○ **More helpful response:** "Is there positive feedback I might be ignoring? Why might I

not believe something positive that somebody says about me?"

- **Mind Reading**

You believe that you know what another person is thinking. Typically this involves arbitrarily deciding that someone is reacting negatively to you.
Example: You are talking to a group of people about your experiences, and notice that one of the people is continually looking at her watch. You assume that she is bored and can't wait for you to stop talking.
  - **More helpful response:** "Am I assuming I know what others are thinking? Am I jumping to conclusions? What's the evidence? Those are my own thoughts, not theirs. Is there another, more balanced way of looking at it?"

- **Fortune Telling**

You believe that things will turn out badly in the future, and are convinced that your predictions are actual   facts.
Example: You decline an invitation to a party, because you think that you will have a terrible time.
  - **More helpful response:** "Do I really believe that I can predict the future? How likely is my prediction to happen?"

- **Catastrophizing**

  You believe the worst possible outcome will occur. Or you think that things can't be any worse. **Example:** You decide against entering in a cooking competition because you believe that if you lose you will be humiliated and none of your friends will ever want to eat your food again.
    - ○ **More helpful response:** "What's actually most likely to happen? In a past similar situation, did my worst fears occur? For a current situation: Is this as bad as it could be? That is, could it be worse?"

- **Magnifying or Minimizing**

  You exaggerate the significance of certain things (such as your mistakes or other people's successes) and minimize other things (such as your own positive qualities or other's imperfections). **Example:** You enter and win a cooking competition. When people compliment you, you demur by replying that your dish actually wasn't one of your best, and didn't they notice that your presentation could have been better?
    - ○ **More helpful response:** "Am I exaggerating the good aspects of others, and putting myself down? Or am I exaggerating the negative and minimizing the positives? How would someone else see it?"

- **Emotional Reasoning**

You assume that the way you feel reflects the way things are. You feel guilty, and therefore believe that you have truly done something bad. Or you feel overwhelmed, and conclude that your problem is truly impossible to solve.
Example: You avoid trying out a new recipe because it looks complicated. The complexity makes you feel anxious, which in turn leads you to believe that the dish is impossible for you to successfully make.
   ○ **More helpful response:** "Just because it *feels* bad, doesn't necessarily mean it **is** bad. My feelings are just a reaction to my thoughts. Where is the evidence that once I start in on the recipe, it won't go better than I originally thought?"

- **"Shoulds"**

You believe things must or must not be a certain way. "Shoulds" act as inflexible rules and standards about the way the world is supposed to work.
Example: As a woman, I should look a certain way, or others won't find me attractive. ("Shoulds" aimed at yourself can lead to feelings of guilt.)
Example: A real man shouldn't cry. I can't believe my boyfriend cried during that movie! ("Shoulds" directed toward others may lead to disappointment, anger, or resentment.)

o **More helpful response:** "What kind of pressure am I putting on myself? Am I setting up expectations for myself or others that are impossible to meet? What would be more realistic standards for myself? For others?"

- **Labeling/Mislabeling**

Sometimes, when you have made a mistake, you get angry at yourself and call yourself a bad name. That is, instead of focusing on what you actually did, you give yourself a label that reflects your entire being. Some common labels are "idiot," "stupid," "good-for-nothing," and "ugly." **Example:** Your pie comes out too sweet because you mis-measured the sugar. For doing so, you call yourself "a loser."
  o **More helpful response:** "Am I labeling myself? Is it fair to sum up my entire existence with one word? Can I explore how I am much more than a single term? Why do I need to beat myself up for making a mistake?"

- **Personalization**

You see yourself as responsible for events around you that you have no control over. This often leads to deep guilt. The other side of this distortion is externalization: this is when you believe that other people have complete control of your life, whereas you have none. This results in blaming others for your situation, while not recognizing the role you are   playing.

Example: Your child is bullied at school. You immediately blame yourself for what happened.

- o **More helpful response:** "Am I jumping to conclusions about my role in an incident? How do I know that I was responsible for what happened? Where is the evidence?"

Example: Every time you watch a certain reality TV show featuring wealthy people, you feel inadequate about your life and become depressed.

- **More helpful response**: "How much power am I giving this TV show over my feelings? How am recognizing my choice whether or not to watch this program?"

Exercise

For the next week, pay attention to what you tell yourself each day. See which things really set off your inner monologue. Notice the connection between something happening and subsequent negative emotions such as guilt, shame, sadness or frustration. At that moment, do an internal check-in and listen closely to what you are saying to yourself. Based on the list of cognitive distortions above, see which categories your negative thinking falls into.

In your journal, I would like you to write down some examples of your negative thinking, along with their categories (for example, mind-reading or catastrophizing).

For each negative thought, please consider the following two questions:

Does this support me or help me achieve my goals in life? Or does this line of thinking create pain?

Additional journal questions

- Where might you have learned the self-talk that goes on in your head?
- When you have a thought about yourself or your life, how do you know that what you are thinking is absolutely true?
- If your self-talk was influenced by another person, could there have been something going on in that person's life that affected how she or he talked to you?
  - What reasons can you think of to support the idea that that person's view of the world is the "right one" for you?

More ways to challenge your irrational thoughts

When something happens that triggers your negative thoughts and begins to make you feel bad about yourself or anxious about a situation, it is up to you recognize what is happening and refuse to be held hostage by your thinking.

The key is to take a time out. Stop, pause, and draw a deep breath. Notice how your thinking is affecting your emotions. If you see that you are engaging in negative thinking, silently tell yourself to "Stop it." You can use a calm voice to do so, or you can shout down those negative voices in an assertive, tough tone. If it is more helpful, you can visualize a large Stop sign that halts your irrational thoughts in their tracks. The important thing is to immediately cut off or drown out any irrational thoughts that have made an appearance. Then ask yourself, "Am I responding appropriately to the situation? Or am I having a knee-jerk reaction that is based on my past experiences? How rational is my thinking here?"

Show yourself some compassion and remind yourself that you don't have to react automatically to a situation. It is perfectly fine to step back and deliberate how to respond. As you will see, there are some powerful questions you can ask yourself that will take the wind out of the sails of your negative thoughts.

The list below provides you with over twenty questions that can help you refute your irrational thoughts. You don't have to memorize all of them. Rather, go through the list and choose four or five that resonate with you. Those will be your go-to questions to ask yourself in order to determine whether or not your thinking is accurate and fair.

- What am I reacting to?
- What do I think is going to happen here?
- What's the worst (and best) that could happen? What's most likely to happen?
- How helpful is it for me to think this way?
- Am I getting things out of proportion?
- Are these negative feelings worth it?
- How important is this really? How important will it be next week? Next month? In 6 months?
- What meaning am I giving this situation?
- Am I overestimating things?
- Am I underestimating my ability to deal with this situation?
- Is there another way I could look at this?
- What could be influencing my interpretation of the situation?
- What advice would I give to a friend in this same situation?
- How much of this situation is within my control? What is outside my control?
- How can I address – even in a small way – things that are under my control?
- What will be the consequences of reacting the way I typically do?
- Could there be another way of dealing with this?
- What would be the most helpful thing to do right now?
- Right now, what is the most effective action I can take?

- What is the evidence that supports my thinking? What is the evidence against it?
- How logically am I thinking this through?
- Am I thinking in a black and white manner?
- Is my source of information trustworthy?
- Would somebody else come to the same conclusions I have?
- Is my thought really 100% true?
- How do I know this thought is really true?

The "should" trap

Especially watch out when the word "should" runs through your head. A "should" or "should not" typically refers to an inflexible rule or a rigid way of viewing reality. This kind of thinking limits you and causes suffering because it is not responsive to the present moment. Instead, it is based on some standard that was created in another time and place. This leads to you feeling pressure, and then guilt, if you can't measure up to the "should."

For example:

- I shouldn't have made that mistake
- I should have known that answer
- I should always keep my home clean and tidy
- I should get married and have children
- I should always be on time
- I should spend more time at work
- I should buy that item because it's on sale
- I should exercise three times a week
- I shouldn't eat between meals

- I should eat that kind of food because it is healthy for me
- I shouldn't have eaten that donut because I should have known better

Of course, some "shoulds" are good for you. Ones like "I should brush my teeth" or "I shouldn't stay up all night" do lead you in the direction of health. That is why it is important to spend time considering which of your "should" statements reflect beliefs that do – or do not – serve your best interests.

Journal questions

- What are your "shoulds"? Please take some time to think about this. Consider some of the rules you have in your life about how you (and other people) should or shouldn't behave. As you come up with them, list each one out.
- From whom or what did you learn each of your "shoulds"?
- How does each of your "shoulds" benefit your life?
- How does each of your "shoulds" limit your life?
- Are there any "shoulds" that it is time to retire?
- Are there any "shoulds" to add to your list that you feel empower you?

Positive Self-Talk

By disputing your irrational thoughts, you will be able to see situations more objectively. This prevents you from being sucked into negative emotions. But that isn't the end of the story. It is vital that you be able to replace your negative thinking with thoughts that are positive and affirming. This is because you will encounter challenges and stresses as you go through life. Stress is part of living that we all have to deal with, so you shouldn't seek to avoid it. Rather, your goal is to be able to handle stressful or new or negative situations in a healthy productive way. Your positive self-talk will get you through difficult times and help you to avoid the suffering caused by irrational thinking. By improving your outlook, you will be able to better handle stress and uncertainty in your life.

An easy way to come up with positive self-talk is to ask yourself what a good friend would say to you about the situation you're dealing with. Think about words that would support and encourage you, make you feel safe and validated, and that would motivate you.

Here are some examples of switching out negative thinking with positive self-talk:

- **Instead of** "I'm scared because I've never done this before," **reframe it** as "This is a chance for me to learn something new."
- Instead of "This is too hard for me. I'm giving up," reframe it as "This is unfamiliar to me right now. I will see which of my friends I can ask for help."
- Instead of "I don't have enough money to travel. Just forget it," reframe it as "I will brainstorm ideas

to make my trip happen. Maybe there are some ways to find the resources that I haven't thought of yet."

- Instead of "This change in my life is pretty scary; I feel powerless," reframe it as "I will do my best to prepare myself for this change."
- Instead of "I'm afraid that I won't be able to handle the stress of living in a new city," reframe it as "I will cross those bridges when I come to them."
- Instead of "I feel like I don't have any friends," reframe it as "What can I do from my end to begin to meet new people? Are there any groups or clubs I'm interested in that I can join?"
- Instead of "Learning this skill is frustrating," reframe it as "Why don't I take a break and come back to this later? That way I'll feel fresh."
- Instead of "I just can't do this," reframe it as "What can I do or learn to ensure that I will be able to do this?"
- Instead of "Look at everyone else – they are much better than I am," reframe it as "Considering my level of training, I think I'm doing fine. I'll get to their level as long as I continue to practice."
- Instead of "I'm really nervous about my piano recital tonight – I don't want to go," reframe it as "Let me just focus on what is happening in each moment and let go of projecting into the future. All I have control over is what is happening right now. I'm just going to keep breathing to keep myself grounded, and I'll be fine."

I also recommend that you develop an all-purpose saying or mantra that you can use to get you through a tough time. One of my favorites is "This too shall pass." I use it when I feel that there is no end in sight to something that is disturbing me. But because I know that everything changes, I make sure to remind myself that nothing – whether good or bad – lasts forever.

The phrase "What can I learn from this?" also regularly helps me find the silver lining in an otherwise negative situation.

Another idea is to hum part of your favorite inspirational song when you are feeling down. For me, Bob Marley's song "Three Little Birds" is a sweet, inspirational tune. When something happens that bothers me, singing the lyrics *"Don't worry about a thing, 'cause every little thing is gonna be alright"* to myself always makes me feel better.

Journal Exercise

- Brainstorm some examples of phrases you could say to yourself when you need to short-circuit a negative thought.
- If you had to choose a single all-purpose saying as your "feel-better-about-life mantra", what would it be?
- Which songs instantly change your mood and lift your spirits when you hear them?

Positive Affirmations

An affirmation is a positive statement that you declare to be true. It refers to an aspect of your life that you would like to develop or something you would like to have happen in your life. Even though an affirmation is future-oriented (because it hasn't occurred yet), what makes it special is that you speak or write it *as if it were currently true*. That is what gives it its power, and allows it to ripen and manifest in your life.

When you were a child, you were on the receiving end of affirmations. That is, the people around you – who didn't necessarily have your best interests at heart – gave you repeated messages, which you soaked up like a sponge. Those messages were things that people "declared to be true" about you and about life. That is why those affirmations played a role in forming your core belief system, which in turn provided the basis for your negative thinking.

Because you are now re-seeding your mind as an adult, it pays to spend time carefully crafting your affirmations. This is your chance to undo those negative messages you received as a youngster that have influenced your life and how you live it. So first, consider your intentions. What would you like to create in your life? What are important qualities you would like to possess? How would you ideally like to be in the world? What changes are important for you to make?

When you choose an affirmation that resonates with you, and then repeat it to yourself, you have the opportunity to slowly but surely change your belief system and how you think about yourself and the world.

This is a sacred time for you, as it finally has become your turn to give yourself the affirmations that you know in your soul are good for you. What will give your positive statements their power is the following very significant (but simple) rule: **What you focus on, grows.**

Examples of affirmations:

- I am grateful for all I have in my life.
- My mistakes are valuable because I learn from them.
- I choose foods that make me feel good.
- I enjoy moving my body.
- I am open to what the world has to offer.
- I am willing to make changes in my life.
- Life's challenges help me grow.
- I enjoy challenging myself.
- I am leading a balanced life.
- I am able to roll with changes.
- I can be comfortable with uncertainty.
- I am able to listen to my body.
- I appreciate my body.
- I enjoy fresh foods.
- I deserve to be loved.
- I respect myself.
- I ask for what I need.
- I dedicate time to being creative.
- I spend quality time alone every week.
- I am committed to being kind to myself.
- I honor and accept all of my emotions
- I trust the wisdom of my body.

- I am grateful for my body.
- I am worthy of love and respect exactly as I am.
- My self-worth is independent of other people's judgments.
- I accept myself exactly as I am in this moment.
- I deserve love exactly as I am in this moment.
- I am worthy simply because I exist.

Here are some tips to get you started on creating your own affirmations:

1. Always use the present tense, as if the affirmation were already true. ("I enjoy spending quality time with my children" instead of "I *will* enjoy spending quality time with my children.")
2. No negatives! Always use the positive form of the idea you are after. (That is, "I feel at peace" is better than "I do not feel stressed.")
3. Be specific. (It helps if your affirmation is measurable, so you'll know when you achieve it)
4. Be realistic. (You don't want your subconscious to have a reason to reject your affirmation)
5. Make your affirmations short and simple to remember. (especially if you'll be writing them down)
6. You can choose to create as many affirmations as you like, but don't overwhelm yourself.
7. Your affirmations should make you feel good inside!

The best way to ensure that affirmations sink into your subconscious is to repeat them. That is why it is helpful to create a daily ritual during which you practice your affirmations. Common times are either upon awakening or before going to bed. The important thing is to be consistent.

You can say your affirmations out loud, repeat them silently in your mind, or write them down. Some people find that stating them while looking into a mirror is particularly powerful. Others find that writing an affirmation over and over again on piece of paper allows it to quickly take hold.

Another idea is to incorporate your affirmations into artwork. In particular, collage is an effective medium because of all the wonderful images you can find in magazines to support your intentions. You could also write your affirmations on index cards and carry them with you, looking at them throughout the day. What is important is that you *own* your affirmations. They are the perfect antidote to negativity, and will foster a positive sense of change in your life.

In the end, the more aware you are of your thought processes, the more control you will have over them. And with more control comes a sense of empowerment – you will no longer be at the mercy of negative beliefs or thoughts that force you into making decisions about food and eating that you would later regret. Instead, control over your mind will give you the ability to make deliberate, conscious decisions about what and how you will eat.

Chapter 9

Skill #6: Disarming "The Inner Critic"

Connected to negative belief systems and cognitive distortions is the "inner critic." This refers to that destructive voice in your head that offers judgmental commentary, usually on a regular basis. It puts you down, makes you feel bad about yourself, keeps you stuck. Accordingly, the inner critic prevents you from making positive changes in your life.

The way you can tell the difference between your inner critic voice and your irrational thinking voice is by how each one addresses you. The following are examples of irrational thinking.

"I shouldn't ask that guy out. He might turn me down."

"I'm afraid to travel abroad, since I might get sick."

"He must think I'm stupid for asking that question."

"Life never turns out the way I want it to."

"I feel guilty that I ate that food; I should've known better."

Notice that these are in the first person ("I") and third person ("he/she/it"). With irrational thinking, you will have the sense that you are truly talking to yourself, or that you are making a statement about life that is not coming from an obvious outside source (such as a parent or teacher).

You can always tell the inner critic, however, because it addresses you using the second person ("you"). It feels like there is actually someone or something else in your mind who is speaking to you with a sense of judgment. And the way your inner critic usually talks is with a strong emotional charge, such as venom, condescension, or disappointment.

"You can't do anything right!"

"Who do you think you are, wanting to apply for that job?"

"See how lazy you are!"

"Wow, you really have gained a lot of weight. You look fat."

"You're an idiot for eating that! You have no self-control!"

"I can't believe you did that. What a loser."

Your inner critic is based on an outside person or thing that has taken up residence in your mind. This is what makes it so destructive – it's as if there is a parasite living inside you, draining your energy and zest for life. There are a number of different ways in which the inner critic works:

- It accepts nothing less than perfection
- It (negatively) evaluates everything you do
- It tries to control – through shaming - your desires and behaviors

- It emphasizes that you are not working hard enough
- It demeans you and undermines your self-confidence by attacking your self-worth
- It attacks your fundamental right to exist
- It makes you feel guilty about things you have done in the past
- It points out – and over-emphasizes – mistakes you have made
- It pushes you to take on a role that is not natural for you (such as being a care-giver or protector)

There is hope, however! Here are four steps you can take that will assist you in neutralizing this negative force.

Step 1: Understand who your critic is. First you must get a sense of the origin of this force that is so quick to judge you. Sometimes, this is the only step necessary for de-fanging an inner critic. This is because once you recognize your critic for who it really is, it will become easy to ignore or blow off.

Please answer the following questions in your journal:

When you were young:

- Whose approval did you value most?
- Whom did you want to impress?
- From whom did you want to hear the words "I value you"?
- Why did you need to hear that?

- Was there somebody in your life who criticized or judged you? Did it happen repeatedly or just once? What were the circumstances? How did it make you feel when it occurred?

Today:

- Whose approval do you value most?
- Whom do you want to impress?
- From whom do you want to hear the words "I value you"?
- Why do you need to hear that?

Take some time to get a sense of who your critic is. Pay close attention to where its voice is coming from inside your body. Is it a parent? A teacher? A monster?

Step 2: Get in touch with what your critic is telling you.

As you go through your day, notice when your critic makes an appearance. What are you doing when it speaks to you? When it does, what does it say to you? What kind of language does it use? How does it speak to you? Does it whisper? Scream? Demand? Cajole? Ridicule? What patterns are you noticing? Write your observations in your journal.

Step 3: Recognize the rationale behind your critic.

Believe it or not, your inner critic sometimes has a positive intent. That is, in its own way, it is doing its best to help you avoid pain. For example, it might want to protect you from failure or rejection. Or it might want to assist you in gaining approval or attention from others. It also could be trying to prevent you from hurting yourself or being too vulnerable.

On the other hand, your inner critic may be the internalized voice of somebody close to you who said mean things to you when you were a child. Either way, it is important for you to be clear about the intention of your inner critic.

If you don't already know, the best way to find out the intention of your inner critic is to ask it directly. Here is an exercise that will allow you to do that:

Find a quiet place where you can be undisturbed. Allow yourself to become centered. You can close your eyes if you wish. Take a deep breath as you give yourself permission to access your inner critic. Have your journal and pen or pencil handy.

1. Allow you mind to soften and think back to the last time your inner critic judged you. Allow yourself to get a clear picture in your mind of how it appeared or might have appeared to you. Begin to pay attention to its details.
2. When you are ready, take a break, and give the inner critic form by drawing it in your journal. Don't worry about your skill as an artist, just try your best. Be sure to include:
   a. Its size, form, color(s), shape, and texture
   b. Any other identifying characteristics
3. Put your pen or pencil down and refocus your attention on the inner critic's presence in your body or mind. Request permission to speak with it. If you

do gain permission, please ask the following questions:
- a. Where did you come from?
- b. Why do you judge me?
- c. What do you want from me?
- d. How did you help me in the past?
- e. How do you currently help me?
- f. How can you help me in the future?
- g. How do you keep me stuck?
- h. What can you teach me?
4. When you are done communicating with your critic, journal on the following:
    - a. What key insights did you gain from your responses to the above questions?
    - b. Were there other feelings/thoughts that came up for you as you brought form to your inner critic?
    - c. Think about what made the critic so fearsome when you were younger. Are those same fears valid now that you are an adult?
    - d. How might your insights help you move forward?

Step 4: Decide what to do about your inner critic.

There are several ways you can deal with your inner critic. If you have discovered that your critic actually does have a positive intent, then it will be healing to dialogue with it. You can return to a conversation with your inner critic in order to negotiate or make peace with it. It is always beneficial to ask your critic what it is afraid might happen if it didn't harangue you.

For example, if your critic is a perfectionist, maybe it believes that if it didn't pick on you, then you would fail in life. So it means well; it is just going about things in a wrong-headed manner. Or a critic who is always preventing you from meeting new people is really trying to protect you from rejection.

Knowing this information will allow you to work together with your critic, so that you can encourage it to take on another, less problematic, role within your psyche. Ideally, you can thank it for caring so much about you, and then reassure it that its concerns aren't valid anymore because of the resources you now have as an adult. Then you can gently escort it to a distant corner of your psyche, where it will be out of the way. Or you and your critic can come up with other ways of looking out for you that don't involve criticizing or judging. That is, perhaps your critic can use their characteristics to assist you in a healthy, productive way.

If, on the other hand, your inner critic is the internalized voice of a parent or caregiver who simply was mean, then it is a wise decision to banish or exorcise it from your psyche.

As you consider what to do about an inner critic who really needs to go, here is a question for you to consider:

- Why might you be willing to continue to internalize the voice of a person from your past who did not have your best interests at heart?

Getting rid on an inner critic is not easy, since it has lived with you for so long. But it can be done. It is necessary that you use your creativity to figure out a powerful ritual in which you can say "Good-bye" to it. One option is to create an imaginary funeral or go through a divorce from it. You could also bury, burn, or destroy a piece of artwork that represents your inner critic. Some people find that writing a letter to their inner critic is an effective way of banishing it. Just the act of writing the letter can be healing. When it is finished, it is up to you what to do with it. As with artwork representing the inner critic, you could do something physically to the letter in a ritual. Or you could simply keep it in a special place.

The key is to plan and complete a ceremony with the intention of releasing the critic from its privileged place in your mind and psyche. After all, now that you are an adult you have much more power than you did when you were younger. You know now that it doesn't serve your best interests to give someone so mean-spirited a place in your life. After all, what makes your critic so special? Were they themselves perfect? What gave them the right to judge you? As Jesus so poignantly spoke (in the gospel of John) to his disciples who wanted to condemn a woman of adultery, *"Let he who is without sin throw the first stone."*

Thus, when you are able to recognize that that your inner critic is not perfect and was just a person – like you – then you can tap into the determination to release its grip from your psyche. Ideally, the clarity you gain about your inner critic is enough to unmask, and unseat, it. It's like Dorothy pulling back the curtain and discovering that the Wizard is really a bumbling little man. All it takes is your intention to move in that direction.

I do, however, want to spend some time discussing how to deal with an inner critic who is a parent. This can be difficult because children often grow up with conflicting feelings:

- I love my mother. She's my mother! I'm supposed to love her. She's supposed to love me.
- She abused me. She told me she wished I'd never been born. Then she told me she loved me. I'm confused.

The first thing to do is recognize that your parent was dealing with their own issues, which influenced how they treated you. Now, this absolutely does not excuse their behavior. I want to be clear about that. If a parent abused you, physically, mentally, emotionally or sexually, then of course that was wrong. At the same time, however, it is important for you to recognize that parents often are dealing with their own demons that their children have no way of understanding. Your parent was only human, doing the best they could with what they had. In my therapy practice, I often find that abusers were themselves abused as children. Therefore, they never learned how to give and receive love in a healthy manner.

The important thing is that the pain a parent (as internalized critic) continues to inflict on you needs to end now. And that means making peace with the past. Not necessarily forgiving – that is up to you. Rather, what is healing is acknowledging that it is time to move forward because what is done is done.

You can begin to move in that direction by writing a letter to your parent-critic (even if they have passed away). Tell them how you felt growing up. Pour your emotions onto the page. Express how their criticism of you has continued to occupy space in your mind. If there was something you needed from them when you were a child, ask for it (not that you will receive it. However, just being able to ask – which you probably couldn't do when you were young – can be powerful). When you are finished with the letter, follow your intuition as to what to do with it. I favor rituals, such as burning, burying or tearing. Think about something symbolic you could do with the letter that would bring you peace about the fact that a parent has been your critic.

As you think about the role of your parent in your life, consider focusing on memories of them being kind and loving, and release the memories of them being dysfunctional and judgmental. This doesn't mean forgetting about how they treated you. Rather, it is choosing to shift your focus away from their negative hold on you. You are much more powerful now that you are an adult. Perhaps you can see that by internalizing their critical voices, you now are victimizing yourself a second time around. It was bad enough that it happened once, in real time. But the fact that you have had to carry them around as an inner critic means that you have truly suffered enough. However you choose to do so, whether with a letter or some kind of ritual, lightening your load will make a profound difference in your life.

Your Advocate

Sometimes it is difficult to truly banish your inner critic. No matter what you do, it continues to be a presence in your mind. But please do not worry. There is an effective way to shut your inner critic down when it makes an appearance.

The key is to have a response ready the next time you are assailed by your inner critic. And that response will come from your **advocate**, whose job is to protect you from the inner critic. Your advocate is an anti-critic; it serves you by providing comfort and uplifting support. It helps you create strong, healthy boundaries that protect you from negativity. It cares deeply about you, and has your best interests at heart. No matter what, it is always in your corner. Your advocate knows you are doing the best you can – after all, nobody is perfect – and it seeks to defend you when you are being unfairly attacked by anyone, especially your inner critic.

Your advocate can appear as a person or animal. Actually, it can take any form at all, as long as it resonates with you. The important thing is that you be able to connect with its positive, affirming energy.

Exercise for finding your advocate

Set aside some time when you won't be disturbed. Make yourself comfortable, either sitting up or laying down, but keep you journal handy. Take some deep breaths and center yourself. Closing your eyes, relax and focus on clearing your mind. As you do so, tell yourself, "I am looking for my advocate. I am looking for my protector. I am looking for someone or something that will support me and that cares for me unconditionally. I will be patient and wait for it to appear."

Let your intuition lead the way. Notice what comes into your mind's eye. See if you can get a sense of your advocate. Be patient as you notice what form coalesces in your imagination...What does it look like? What is its energy like? Does it have a message for you? What kinds of things will it say and/or do in order to challenge your inner critic? How will it defend – and encourage – you?

When you are ready, re-orient yourself and write what you experienced in your journal.

You might like to make a drawing or painting of your advocate. You can create an image of your advocate using other forms of art, such as clay or collage if you like. You could even write a poem about it.

Another option is to choose an object that represents your advocate, and carry it with you during the day. By having it close, the energy of your advocate will always be by your side.

I would like you to practice accessing your advocate during the day. Your goal is to quickly be able to utilize that imagery/energy whenever the inner critic makes an appearance. As soon as your inner critic tries to judge you, your advocate can challenge it and shut it down. This way, the inner critic can be managed, and your psyche – that part of you that is being criticized – will be protected. Your advocate can also serve as a mentor, and provide you with guidance if you need it, or assist you in developing an action plan for something you'd like to undertake.

***

By following *The Buddha Diet*, you are doing something new for yourself. You are stretching your comfort zone. Anytime a person does this, it impacts their belief system, which can trigger negative thinking. Add in the inner critic, and it is easy to see why it is easy to become discouraged and return to old ways of living. After all, it is difficult to start new behaviors when you are assailed by thoughts that challenge your every move.

Your relationship with food and eating developed over many years. Since you have had to eat multiple times a day, it makes sense that any changes in your daily habits could be threatening to your world view. My hope is that the information in the preceding three chapters has helped you recognize dysfunctional mental processes, and assisted you in maintaining your commitment to reshaping the manner in which you eat.

Chapter 10

Skill #7: Managing Emotional Eating

Ordinarily we don't let ourselves experience ourselves fully. We have a fear of facing ourselves. Many people try to find a spiritual path where they do not have to face themselves but where they can still liberate themselves. In truth, that is impossible. We have to be honest with ourselves. We have to see our gut, our real shit, our most undesirable parts.

Chogyam Trungpa Rinpoche

The quieter you become, the more you can hear.

Ram Dass

Where you stumble, there lies your treasure.

Joseph Campbell

...and that ties in with what the Native Americans say, which is that there is always a story being told to you by every situation – and every object that you're surrounded by is telling you something if you start to look carefully.

Genesis P-Orridge

We usually think of "emotional eating" as using food to suppress or soothe a feeling we are having (or are about to have). It truly is amazing to consider the many reasons why we may eat when we're not physically hungry:

- To distract ourselves
- To comfort ourselves
- To sedate ourselves
- To punish (ourselves and/or others)
- To protect ourselves from unwanted attention (for example, weight gain)
- To regulate an out-of-whack biological system
- To instigate care-giving responses from others
- To keep others at a distance
- To give the illusion of being in control (for example, anorexia)
- To self-medicate against the pain, anxiety, rage, fear, and somatic distress caused by a traumatic experience

Plus, there are a multitude of other things that can trigger emotional eating:

- o Boredom
- o Loneliness
- o Procrastination
- o Self-reward/bribery
- o Excitement
- o Love
- o Frustration
- o Anger
- o Sadness
- o Stress
- o Anxiety
- o Hatred
- o Depression

In chapter three you learned how to recognize when you are physically hungry. If you have a history of emotional eating, however, it might be challenging to give up that habit because it is such a deep part of your life. I do believe you can begin to heal from emotional eating **if** you pay close attention to its presence in your life. The key is to avoid resisting emotional eating until you are ready to give it up. Don't just force yourself to stop. For now, I would just like you to practice noticing when you desire food. Be curious. Follow your compulsions. Explore and examine the feelings that lead to your urge to use food for something other than physical hunger. Those moments when you are craving food to deal with an emotional issue are actually quite valuable. That is because emotional eating indicates that there is a deep need begging to be met. Thus, the symptom is a visible signal for you to pay attention to some core truth or wound. In that sense, it is a sacred call for self-transformation.

So whatever the reason or the trigger, I would like you to view emotional eating as a gift. This is because your habit is a divine wake-up call, serving as a guide to show where you need look to find the pain and then to heal.

At this point, don't worry about getting rid of emotional eating or manipulating it. Your main job is working to *understand* your behavior. The compulsion to eat when not hungry is a signal for you to pay attention to your emotional truth. In that sense, emotional eating has a deep, compelling personal meaning for each person. What is most important is for you to be kind to yourself and not judge yourself for emotional eating. After all, if you had a more compelling alternative for dealing with emotions, you'd already be utilizing it!

Instead, be open to the message that your emotional eating is sending. Only then is change possible. I believe that at the bottom of every person's emotional eating, there is pain. Discovering and engaging with that pain will allow a person to resolve what needs to be resolved, and thereby end the compulsion to emotionally eat.

To begin, let's explore why **food** might be your preferred method of dealing with emotions.

Journal Exercise

1. What are your first memories of eating food when you weren't physically hungry?
2. Did you learn how to use food in that way on your own, or from somebody else?

3. Currently, what does emotional eating do for you that is valued or needed in your world?
4. To what problem is emotional eating a solution, or an attempt at a solution?
5. How has emotional eating been an actual success for you, rather than a failure?
6. What would happen if you stopped using food to handle your emotions? What are you afraid of happening?

Please fill in the following:

I engage in emotional eating for a specific purpose:

Based on what you just wrote, would you agree with the following sentence? Why or why not?

"For me, achieving this purpose is worth the specific pain and troubles that accompany emotional eating."

Noticing patterns

One way to begin understanding your emotional eating and the roots of your cravings is to keep a food diary (first introduced in Chapter 3). Doing so will help you discover the links between when and why you are eating. You'll also become more aware of exactly how much food you are consuming. As the days go by, it will be interesting (and illuminating) for you to notice what patterns emerge.

Your food diary can be a wonderful tool, because it will force you to slow down and really think about your food and eating habits. For example, you might come to notice that on the days you have a large dinner, the next day you are likely to skip breakfast, and then desperately crave sugar mid-morning. Or that every time you get off the phone with a particular relative, you feel the need to grab something sweet. Or that on Sundays you eat more junk food than on other days of the week.

Once you are able to clearly understand when and why you are eating the way you do, you will b able to figure out effective strategies for addressing eating habits that you'd like to change.

You can keep your food diary in any kind of notebook, large or small. You could also use a digital device like a computer, tablet or smartphone if that is easier. Just make sure it is convenient for you to carry around and write in.

In your food diary (which should also include any beverages you consume), you will record the following information:

1. Time of day and location
2. Hunger level (based on the Hunger Scale)
3. Your mood (and why you are in that mood)
4. The food that you decided to eat
5. How much food you ate
6. How you felt during your meal
7. How you felt after the meal:
   a. Physically
   b. Emotionally

Keep your food diary for at least one month. This is not necessarily a time of change for you. Rather it is one of exploration. So be curious and be patient. When you are ready to change, you will! In the next section, you will learn what to do when you are ready to address your cravings.

Dealing with Compulsion

Urges behave like waves – they start small, build to a crest, then break up and dissolve. When you urge surf, you ride the wave rather than fight it; as a result, you are less likely to be pulled in or wiped out.

Susan Nolen-Hoeksema

When you find yourself craving food, it is time to use your mindfulness skills. Awareness is the key that will help you figure out what is initiating your desire to eat. First you must ask yourself whether you are physically hungry. Use the hunger scale to check in with yourself. It could also be that your cravings are physically-based. Low blood sugar, hormonal imbalances, adrenal fatigue, and vitamin, mineral or protein deficiency can all lead to strong urges for particular foods. As you begin to make particular changes in your diet (for example, cutting out sugar or eating more fish), you may begin to notice that your cravings diminish. Your food diary will be a handy way for you to explore those connections.

On the other hand, you might be metaphorically hungry for something else. By paying attention to your body, you may notice that there is a hole – whether in your belly or in your heart or in your soul – that you need to fill with food. This is when I would like you to take a step back and observe (non-judgmentally) the emotion you are feeling, and then describe it to yourself.

"I am starting to get angry." "I feel sad." "I am lonely." "My stress is beginning to overwhelm me." "I'm bored and just have no idea what to do with myself." "I'm really excited about my date."

Next, utilize your positive self-talk as you have a conversation with yourself, starting with the questions: "Will eating this food really help me deal with this feeling?" and "Will eating food get me closer to what I really want or will it separate me?"

The dialogue you have with yourself as you witness your urge to emotionally eat is vital, as it will influence your ability to discard this behavior and move in a healthier direction.

As you continue to notice your urge to eat, ask yourself:

1. What am I aware of, right now?
   a. What thoughts are going through my mind?
   b. What am I feeling?
2. What do I need, right now?
3. How am I stopping myself from getting it, right now?

This is the time to remember the skills you have learned in previous chapters. When you are connected with your core values and able to tap into your self-compassion, it becomes easier to turn away from going down a path that you know won't serve your interests.

I particularly like the SIFT system developed by author M.J. Ryan, which will allow you to strengthen your "witness self." As you notice your urge to eat, give yourself permission to take a step back. Take a breath and then ask yourself the following questions. They will cause a rupture in your food trance, and allow you to see your situation in a different light.

1. **S**ensations: What are the sensations in my body? (heat, cold, pressure, constriction, expansion) Where are they located?
2. **I**mages: What images are coming up?
3. **F**eelings: What emotions am I experiencing?
4. **T**hinking: What are the stories I am telling myself?

You can use the SIFT method with any kind of compulsion in order to gain enough time to **pause** before you do something you regret. This time-out is something that most people skip when they are craving food. They just move from having a certain feeling to developing a craving to finding food and eating it. It's like having tunnel-vision, with no distractions getting in the way of the craving!

So what will allow you to break your food trance? Your mindfulness and self-talk skills, coupled with your self-compassion, curiosity and connection with your core values.

When you notice you are having a craving, that is the exact time to tell yourself: "I'm aware I'm having an urge to eat. But am I really physically hungry? I guess now I have a moment of decision. Am I going to go down this path? Or am I going to turn away and walk down another path?"

With practice, you will come to understand that moment as an important crossroads. For you already know where one path leads; you've been down it many times before. It seems to make sense in the moment, but it truly never leads anywhere. In fact, it seems to go in a circle, leading back to where you came each time. The other road, however, keeps going forward. It may be unfamiliar to you right now, and while challenging, it does eventually lead to healing and peace. Might you be willing to give it a chance?

Taking control of emotional eating begins when you recognize what is happening and why. That conscious moment of decision, **before** you act on your craving, is the moment of possibility. Your goal must be to fully inhabit that moment, and, if possible, stretch it out so that you can act with deliberation, instead of flipping on your tunnel vision and going into the trance that leads straight to the fridge. In the end, the fact that you recognize that you have a **choice** about what to do about your emotions is what will give you the power to break the apparent monopoly of emotional eating.

But for this to work, you first must be able to understand what you're truly needing in that moment, and then have the ability to get that need met in a healthy way. In chapter 6 you learned about developing self-compassion and honoring your needs and how to meet them. Those are the skills that will enable you to make new choices in that moment of decision before you act on an urge.

It is also true, however, that most people haven't had the opportunity to learn how to manage difficult emotions. And because those emotions are often at the root of emotional eating, that skill is essential to breaking this habit. In the next chapter I will discuss how to handle feelings in a healthy way. For right now, I would just like to focus on using your inner dialogue to help you to learn more about why your food cravings are coming up in the first place.

Besides using SIFT, when you are having the urge to eat, you could use your journal to ask yourself these further questions to gain clarity about your situation.

- What's going on here with this urge to eat?
- Am I being honest with myself?
- How is my compulsion promising to give me relief?
- Will it really?
- What's been my experience using food in the past to find relief?
- What's really bothering me? Why am I feeling this way?
- Could I just allow this feeling to be here without reacting to it? What gets in the way of doing that?
- What do I really need in this moment?
- What is preventing me from getting that need met?
- What can I do in the future to address that need?
- What can I do right now other than emotionally eat?

I hope that the feedback you have gotten from your food diary and journaling is allowing you to gain a deeper understanding of your emotional eating and how that process works in your life. Perhaps that awareness will lead you to discard this habit. However, if you are not yet ready to give up emotional eating, that is fine. After all, until you find better ways of managing emotions, it makes sense to still use it as a coping tool. The key is to remain mindful of what you are doing and why. This is because resisting a habit you are not ready to change will only make it stronger. So please don't feel guilty about engaging in emotional eating! After all, if you had a healthier way to cope, you would use it. I believe that when you are ready, you will change.

I do wonder, though, how the act of using food to manage your emotions would change if you decided to do it with your full, undivided attention. What might you notice?

Emotional eating as spiritual practice

What if you decided to make emotional eating:

- A meditation?
- A ceremony?
- A beautiful experience?
- A chance to honor a "bad habit"?
- An exercise in curiosity?
- An opportunity to be self-compassionate?

Yes, I am actually asking your "honor" your habit of emotional eating! Since you're going to do it anyway, why not own it? Think of this as a chance to truly inhabit your experience of emotional eating, in order to learn how it truly affects you.

So the next time you are going to engage in emotional eating, please do the following:

- Sit down and make yourself comfortable
- Acknowledge the fact that you are eating to deal with an emotion
- Forgive yourself, and then give yourself permission to eat
- Focus on what you are doing
- Go slowly and deliberately
- Be conscious of what you are doing
- Divide the process of preparing your food and eating into as many small acts as possible
- Pay attention to each step of your emotional eating experience.
- Also pay close attention to each bite and how it affects you, both physically and emotionally.

While you are eating, you can ask yourself:

- What kind of relief am I experiencing?
- Does this feel like **love**? (If not, what does it feel like?)

After you are done eating please remember to treat yourself with kindness and compassion. As I said above: At this point, emotional eating might be your best coping tool for emotions and stress. And that's OK. When you find healthier, more empowering ways of coping, you will change. So acknowledge that you are doing the best that you can right now. That means no guilt or remorse! Also, please do not deprive yourself of food the next day in order to make up for what you ate.

Remember that engaging in a compulsion is never wasted time if you can learn from it. Therefore, it might be helpful to take some time to journal about your experience with "mindful" emotional eating.

- How was this experience with emotional eating different than my prior experiences doing it?
- What did I learn about my habit?
- What did I learn about myself?

***

My hope is that you now understand your emotional eating much better than you did before. Since you know this habit does not serve your interests in the long run, perhaps you are truly ready to leave it behind. Now your next step is to discover alternative coping strategies for managing difficult emotions. That is the purpose of the next chapter.

Chapter 11

Skill #8: Dealing with Emotions

There seems to be some connection between the places we have disowned inside ourselves and the key to where we need to go. Life as usual has arranged a way in which we're not allowed to leave anything behind that is not somehow resolved.

David Whyte

The only way to live an authentic life is to explore, acknowledge, and embrace the dark aspects of your soul that compel you to make choices that generate pain and hardship.

David Simon

Every moment you are being born anew. Every moment you die, and every moment you are born. Tremendous changes happen every day. It is a flux. Everything goes on flowing, nothing is frozen. But the mind is a dead thing, it is a frozen phenomenon. If you act from the frozen mind, you live a dead life. You don't live really – you are already in the grave...

Osho

Consider the following four scenarios:

1. Jane is using a hammer as she repairs her fence. She bangs her thumb. She immediately thinks to herself, "I can't believe I just did that. I'm such an idiot." Even though nobody is around, she turns red and gets angry at herself. Continuing to berate herself as she rubs her thumb, she begins to feel depressed and ends up going inside, where she serves herself a big bowl of cereal.

2. Every Wednesday evening Larry's sister Wendy calls him. Wendy has a chronic illness and has been calling Larry regularly for over a year in order to vent. Larry generally doesn't speak much during these conversations, which last about an hour. Larry finds that on Wednesdays he feels out of sorts, and usually doesn't have much of an appetite for dinner.

3. John is a teacher. It's the last day of classes before summer break. He thinks about how much he's going to miss his students. This makes him feel sad. On the way home he stops at the store to pick

up a box of cookies. He knows they'll make him feel better.

4. Laura's father passed away when she was ten years old. At the funeral Laura wanted to cry, but her mother put her hand on her shoulder and said, "Big girls don't cry. Let's be strong, now." For her mother's sake, Laura stifled her tears. Today, as an adult, Laura finds it difficult to respond emotionally when something sad happens. However, she does notice that every so often – apparently at random – she'll feel a heavy sense of sadness wash over her. This disturbs her, so when it happens she distracts herself by heading to the fridge or, if she's out, thinking about her next meal.

In this chapter, I would like to discuss how to handle feelings and emotions (I will be using these two terms interchangeably) in a healthy way. For if you're going to give up using food to manage emotions, then what? There has to be something you can do with your feelings that you won't regret afterwards.

I began with the above scenarios because it is important to recognize that not all emotional landscapes are the same. This means that there will be different strategies for handling emotions, depending on their context. As you will see, some emotions deserve to be honored. Others, not so much.

My goal is for you to be able to understand the place of emotions in your life so that you can **respond** to them appropriately, instead of **react** to them in ways that are not in your best interests. The key skill that makes all the difference in navigating your emotions is mindfulness. For with awareness comes the power to make positive changes. In addition, being able to step into witness consciousness will give you the necessary distance to recognize your internal processes without being completely subsumed by them. Now let's revisit each of the scenarios one by one.

First scenario

Jane is using a hammer as she repairs her fence. She bangs her thumb. She immediately thinks to herself, "I can't believe I just did that. I'm such an idiot." Even though nobody is around, she turns red and gets angry at herself. Continuing to berate herself as she rubs her thumb, she begins to feel depressed and ends up going inside, where she serves herself a big bowl of cereal.

This is a common occurrence for all of us. Look at the following sequence of events:

1. Something happens out of the blue.
2. Your negative thinking or inner critic kicks into gear.
3. You begin experiencing distressing emotions.

As you go throughout your day, random events happen that affect you emotionally. Lousy service at a restaurant. A driver who cuts you off. A friend who doesn't respond to your text. When these things happen, you tell yourself things about the situation that then lead you to feel a certain way.

Solution: You will be able to diffuse your distressing emotions by using the skills you learned in chapters 8 and 9 that focused on negative self-talk and your inner critic. Your choice to show yourself compassion, and your ability to be mindful will allow you to recognize what is happening in the moment and make you aware of the story you are telling yourself. "Life sucks." "This isn't fair." "She must hate me." "I'm so disappointed in myself."

Taking a step back (utilizing your witness consciousness) will give you the opportunity to challenge the voices in your head that are causing your negative feelings. This is also a good time to make use of your positive affirmations or a mantra. "Oh, well – nobody said life is fair." "All I can do is try my best." "I'm not going to let this ruin my day." "I'm not going to let some jerk control my mood." The Serenity Prayer is another handy tool that can put things in perspective for you:

God, grant me the serenity

To accept the things I cannot change,

Courage to change the things I can,

And the wisdom to know the difference.

These kinds of feelings are based on cognitive distortions or your inner critic's monologue. Once you challenge your negative thinking or shut down your inner critic, the emotion should dissipate on its own. As you breathe deeply you will notice how it feels to release the negativity. Then you can shift your focus to something else and move on.

Second scenario

Every Wednesday evening Larry's sister Wendy calls him. Wendy has a chronic illness and has been calling Larry regularly for over a year in order to vent. Larry generally doesn't speak much during these conversations, which last about an hour. Larry finds that after these phone conversations he feels irritable and frustrated. He usually doesn't have much of an appetite for dinner and goes to bed feeling out of sorts.

This is a situation in which feelings are **legitimately** arising in response to an issue that needs to be resolved. That is, instead of being driven by irrational thinking, Larry's feelings are a natural consequence of what he is experiencing. In this case, his feelings are important feedback, telling Larry that something needs to change about the situation. It's as if the feelings are a big red flag, signaling that something isn't right about what is happening.

Another example would be a wife getting angry because her husband doesn't call her when he stays late at the office. Sitting at home alone waiting, she finds it all too easy to have a sugary snack. In this instance, the wife's need to feel like her husband cares enough to phone is not being met, which then naturally leads to anger and frustration.

Fortunately, there are several ways to address these kinds of situations so that they do not provoke distressing feelings.

Solution: First, it is necessary to recognize the connection between negative feelings and the situation that is generating them. Because negative feelings often lead to emotional eating, keeping a food diary will allow you to easily see these patterns. Next, instead of ignoring those feelings or distracting yourself with food, it will be important to spend some time being present with those feelings. They are your allies begging you to pay attention to what is going on. So journaling about them or simply noticing how they unfold will force you to take a closer look at the situation. As you do so, you can contemplate the following important questions:

1. Am I giving away any of my personal power in this situation? How so?
2. How are my boundaries? Is there something I am tolerating or allowing that is not in my best interests?
3. Is this a situation I have any control over? If I do not, how can I change my perspective so that I may make peace with it? If I do have some measure of control, then what is preventing me from getting my needs met? What can I do to strengthen my resolve

to change the situation? Is there somebody or something I can use for support?

4. Where does my responsibility lie in creating and/or maintaining this situation?

If you are having trouble with your boundaries and sticking up for yourself, then it will be helpful for you to return to the chapters on self-compassion and combating negative belief systems and self-talk. This is because when you care deeply about yourself, you won't allow another person to take advantage of you or put you in an uncomfortable situation. You will know that you are worthy of respect and that it is OK to ask that your needs be met. In addition, it will be important for you to address any negative internal dialogue that is preventing you from asserting yourself.

If you find that you have little or no control over the situation (you hate your boss but still have to take meetings with him), then the key is to prepare in advance to manage your negative emotions. After all, this will be something you can predict. So after the distressing situation occurs, you could arrange things so that you are able to:

1. Go exercise
2. Have a nice meal
3. Spend time with friends or family, to whom you can vent
4. Take a drive and listen to your favorite music
5. Read an inspiring book (some people like to look at a passage from the Bible)
6. Take a kick-boxing class
7. Journal
8. Clean your house

9. Garden

It doesn't matter what you do, as long as you can distract yourself from ruminating on negative thoughts and sinking into negative feelings. Some people find that organizing something (their office, kitchen, garage) can be helpful because it gives them a sense of control and satisfaction. Another great tool to use in these kinds of situations is the *Emotional Freedom Technique*, which I will describe below. And one additional thing to consider is volunteering. Assisting people or caring for animals is an easy way to redirect attention and generate positive feelings.

According to the old Chinese proverb:

If you want happiness for an hour, take a nap.

If you want happiness for a day, go fishing.

If you want happiness for a year, inherit a fortune.

If you want happiness for a lifetime, help somebody.

Third Scenario

John is a teacher. It's the last day of classes before summer break. He thinks about how much he's going to miss his students. This makes him feel sad. On the way home he stops at the store to pick up a box of cookies. He knows they'll make him feel better.

In cases like this, something happens that legitimately leads to an emotional reaction. Neither cognitive distortions nor the inner critic play a role here. Nor is the situation a reminder of some past event or an indication that something currently is wrong and thus needs to be changed. Instead, you are simply responding to an event or situation in the present that naturally causes you to feel one or more emotions. Watching a sad movie. Moving from a childhood home. Hearing a piece of bad news. Learning about an injustice in the world. Accidentally forgetting to do something you promised for a friend. Grieving the loss of somebody close to you.

Unfortunately, many of us do not attend to our emotions during these kinds of situations. What do we do instead? Avoid them, deny them, repress them, ignore them...We'll typically do anything so that we won't have to experience a distressing feeling!

It is ironic, however. Even though we often are afraid of being fully present with a feeling, the feeling itself does not have the power to kill us. On the other hand, what we often do to avoid a feeling can cause us great physical and mental harm – and even lead to death. Consider: Drinking alcohol, smoking, drugging, eating, watching TV, staying on the computer for hours at a time.....Each one is a way to distract ourselves when we want to avoid dealing with a feeling. But unless we are willing to be present with our feelings and work through them, they will stay inside of us, causing problems of one kind or another. For if you deny an emotion, you then miss an opportunity to learn what is preventing you from expressing it – and thus aren't able to face a core issue that needs addressing.

Solution: The key is to feel feelings – not avoid them. Emotions are not the enemy! They are natural forms of energy that have been triggered for some reason or another. It is important that you pay attention to your emotions and figure out what to do about them. So no more pretending they aren't there! Instead, I would like you to give yourself permission to own what you're feeling. It is OK to feel sad. It is OK to feel bitter. Or frustrated. Or angry. Or lost. Or happy. It is OK.

By embracing and fully experiencing your feelings, you then gain the power to release them in a healthy way.

My belief is that if you are having a feeling (not based on a cognitive distortion or inner critic), then it is legitimate. That is, if you are feeling something, then it deserves your attention – and should not be ignored. Like water seeking the lowest ground level, emotions also seek expression by moving through you (specifically, by leaving your body). It is an irony that when you fight against feeling a negative emotion, you actually make it stronger, by denying the physical release out of your body which it needs.

Emotions have a natural flow and ebb. You can see that in action by watching a very young child. It is striking how a little one can fully inhabit an emotion like anger or sadness, express it with their whole body, and then move on like nothing had happened. Unfortunately, as we grow up we often learn to either ignore our feelings or do something that interferes with them (such as eat). Instead of letting an emotion pass through us, like an ocean wave, we block its natural course. And as you can imagine, damming something that doesn't want to be hemmed in takes a tremendous amount of physical and soul energy. Therefore, the challenge is to regain that initial sense of freedom when it comes to expressing emotions. Not that you should scream or wail like a three year old. But rather, that you figure out something to do with your emotion that gives it full expression and resolution in a way that is meaningful to you. How to do so? **It is my belief that our intuition always knows what we should be doing with our feelings. The key is to listen to our intuition, and have the courage to follow it.**

So what might happen if you simply committed to be present with an emotion? You might discover that you actually become empowered when you surrender to the moment, face your feeling, and then follow its lead. This is because a feeling will take you deeper into the knowledge of yourself as you remain present with it. If you allow it to direct you to where it wants you to go, then you will discover exactly what you must do to resolve it in a healthy way.

It is also significant that when you remain present with a distressing feeling, you will discover that its discomfort is cyclical, not linear. So as much as you may fear it, the feeling will not last forever! You'll find that after a difficult emotion washes over you, it gently begins to recede. It is similar to the waves of the ocean. The feeling approaches. It gathers steam. It crests. It changes. It dissolves.

This process may take some time – hours or even days. But that is OK, because by simply being present with the ebb and flow, you will notice that what the feeling is asking of you is that you be witness to it. **That you honor it by simply feeling it.** Be certain, however, that your mind stays out of the way. Negative thinking is something that can disrupt the natural flow of a feeling. Ruminating over being angry or sad is certain to keep the feelings from resolving on their own.

But as I mentioned, if you have the faith to follow your intuition, then you'll know what to do with a difficult feeling. Whether you scream, cry, journal, create a memorial, tear something up, or recite the Serenity Prayer – you'll know you're on the right track because you'll notice a sense of peace in your heart.

As you try to tune into your intuition, one of your biggest challenges will be the voice (either from you or others around you) that says to you, "You shouldn't be having this feeling." Or, equally as bad, "Shouldn't you be over this feeling by now?" Those are insidious lines of reasoning. As you remain present with an emotion, you will discover that it will resolve in its own time, not according to some predetermined schedule. Grief is a good example of this. For some people grieving can last for weeks. For others, it can take months and even years. Because each person is different, it is important to allow feelings to manifest and resolve in their own time. This will require your patience and willingness to treat yourself kindly as you remain present with difficult feelings. Often, just telling yourself that you are not going to rush a feeling away is enough to make it bearable, and will lead to its dissolution.

When you decide to become present with a feeling, here are some suggestions of what to do:

o   Sit with it and observe how it feels within you. Just breathe, and allow yourself to be present with your emotion. Be curious about it as it unfolds and transforms itself. That's all you need to do.

- Take a walk and see what you notice.
- Dialogue with it out loud or in your journal.
- Write a letter to it.
- Free-write about it in your journal.
- Write a poem about it.
- Represent it in art (drawing, painting, collage, etc.).

A final suggestion. I have found that the following questions can help to turn a negative situation into an opportunity for self-growth. When something bad happens to you, be sure to embrace your feelings instead of avoiding them. But at the same time, ask yourself:

1. What am I learning from this?
2. What is this preparing me for?
3. Where does my responsibility lie in all this?
4. How is this situation giving me an opportunity to face something I have been avoiding?

As you answer these questions, notice what happens to the emotion(s) you are feeling.

Fourth scenario

Laura's father passed away when she was ten years old. At the funeral Laura wanted to cry, but her mother put her hand on her shoulder and told her, "Big girls don't cry. Let's be strong, now." For her mother's sake, Laura stifled her tears. Today, as an adult, Laura finds it difficult to respond emotionally when something sad happens. However, she does notice that every so often – apparently at random – she'll feel a heavy sense of sadness wash over her. This disturbs her, so when it happens she distracts herself by heading to the fridge or, if she's out, thinking about her next meal.

This scenario involves an emotion that arises because something or someone in the present reminds you of a past situation. In psychology we call that reminder – whether it's a person, place or thing – a "trigger."

Now, it is natural to feel emotions when something causes you to recall a powerful memory from your past. For example, driving by the old house you grew up in and remembering how sad you were when you moved. Or eating Thai food and wistfully recalling your experiences in that country. The issue here is the degree to which you feel the emotions, and whether there is any lingering baggage you are still dragging around in your subconscious.

When we become triggered by something that is still unresolved, we instantly feel strong emotions. Our ability to respond to a situation is thus negatively impacted because we feel overwhelmed. This is known as reactive behavior: we are reacting to the present as if we were still in the past. This means we lose our spontaneity and can't respond to the situation in an appropriate manner. Instead, we might fly off the handle, shut down, or become very depressed. Either way, we are being held hostage in the present by something from our past. However, it is also true that triggers are a goldmine of information and should be respected, because they are telling you about emotional issues that you still need to address and put to rest.

Solution: When something from the past (that has been resolved) brings up strong emotions in the present, it is helpful to simply be present with your feelings and let them naturally unfold. Therefore, following the solutions mentioned above for scenario 3 will be most helpful.

On the other hand, for handling emotions that are based on unresolved issues from the past, it is best to use your mindfulness skills to recognize what is happening to you. As you become aware that you have been triggered, you can pause and give yourself a time out. Then immediately tell yourself:

"This is just a reminder of the past. That was then, and this is now. Even though this memory makes me **feel** upset, it's not **actually** occurring again right now."

The following are helpful questions that will allow you to gain control over your emotions when something in the present reminds you of a past event:

- o   What am I feeling?
- o   What does this remind me of?
- o   What do I need right now?
- o   What can I actually do about the situation?

Next, it will be vital for you to give yourself permission to be open to what you are feeling. Observe it. Many people have been taught that they shouldn't feel certain feelings. For example, a little boy might have learned that crying is only for sissies. Or a girl's mother might have stressed "keeping it together" at family funerals. Or perhaps a child grew up in a family where anger simply wasn't done (at least out in the open).

The key is to turn towards your feelings, to be attentive to them. If you are willing to acknowledge a particular feeling fully and completely, then you will be able to give it what it wants – recognition. And once you recognize a feeling, you will also receive feedback from it, as far as how it needs to be expressed or resolved.

But what gets in the way of embracing a feeling? **Fear**: those voices in your head or beliefs in your heart that push you away from discomfort, telling you that painful things will happen if you are present with your feelings:

- Once you start crying, you'll never stop.
- You're being unreasonable about things.
- You shouldn't be having this feeling, anyway.
- The hurt will be unbearable.
- The truth about the matter is just too much to handle.

Your challenge is to dispute those suppositions. For that is all they are: negative ideas about "reality" that actually are not real. I can't tell you how many people I've worked with in therapy who were afraid that they wouldn't stop crying once they started. And each was truly surprised to learn that eventually they did stop crying – and felt better for the experience.

So once again, this is where the skills you learned in the chapters about negative belief systems, negative thinking, and the inner critic will come in handy. You'll need to have a conversation with yourself in which you argue against the voice that wants the easy way out. Your response must be: "This supposed easy way out (like using food to pull my attention elsewhere) doesn't work! All it does is make me feel lousy afterwards. I'm going to take chance and do something different for a change."

Here are some detailed questions you can ask yourself if you decide to write about your feeling in your journal:

- The times when I usually experience this feeling:
- The way I usually deal with this feeling:
- The place in my body where this feeling lives:
- If this feeling had a color, it would be:
  - Shape:
  - Size:
  - Texture:
  - Temperature:
- If this feeling could talk, it would say:
- What I want to say back to this feeling:
- I block myself from knowing more about this feeling because:
- I am afraid that if I let myself truly feel this feeling, I would:
- How I would like to ideally deal with this feeling:
- A way I could use this feeling productively:
- The three things I am willing to do, starting now, to change my relationship to this feeling are:
- As I work on exploring this feeling, I will ask for support from:

When you are ready, you can also do this same exercise for other feelings that you've had a hard time fully expressing.

What to do next

As you already know, journaling is a powerful way to begin to heal from a painful experience in the past that continues to haunt you. As you think about a negative past experience, please answer the following questions:

- How has this event shaped my life?
- What does this mean within my larger life story?
- How is this part of my journey?
- How might this negative event be the basis for some kind of contribution I might make to the world?
- How might it allow me to deepen my relationships to myself and others?
- How might this negative event now lead me to show myself and others more compassion?
- How has this painful event made me a more sensitive person?

In the end, your intuition will lead you where you must go in order to heal. The skills you have learned in this book will provide you with the faith, courage, and ability to simply listen to your heart and do what you know you need to do.

***

Another tool you can use to address a distressing emotion is something called *Emotional Freedom Technique* (abbreviated as "EFT").

Originally developed by Gary Craig, EFT is a form of energy medicine that uses light tapping with your fingertips to access traditional Chinese medicine acupuncture points on your face and body. By combining this physical tapping with affirmations about an emotional issue, a person can dislodge stuck energy and dissipate painful emotions. This is an easily learned, portable technique that you can use anywhere, anytime.

There is a storehouse of free information about how to do EFT on the internet. All you have to do is google "EFT protocols" and you will discover a wealth of detailed information. What I would like to offer you here is a basic overview. This will be enough to allow you to begin using EFT immediately to address distressing emotions. If you find that this tool resonates with you and provides relief, then I wholeheartedly encourage you to learn more about it. EFT is something I use all the time, both personally and professionally, and am happy to be able to share it with you.

Step 1: You can use EFT with anything that is causing you distress. This includes emotions, cravings, or even physical symptoms. To begin, think about what you are experiencing and measure it on a scale from zero (the problem is gone) to ten (the problem at its most intense). Keep that number in the back of your mind. Being aware of this number and how it changes will give you important feedback while you do EFT.

Next, create an affirmation. The pattern of this statement is always the same:

"Even though [problem or emotion], I love and accept myself."

The more detail you can include, the better.

Examples:

"Even though I feel anxious about my job interview, I love and accept myself."

"Even though I am angry at my friend because of what she said, I love and accept myself."

"Even though I feel sad about missing my friend's birthday, I love and accept myself."

"Even though I am stressed out about my job, I love and accept myself."

"Even though I feel depressed because it's the anniversary of my parent's death, I love and accept myself."

"Even though this memory of my father makes me angry, I love and accept myself."

"Even though I am craving donuts, I love and accept myself."

"Even though I have a headache, I love and accept myself."

"Even though I can't fall asleep, I love and accept myself."

You can also use EFT to address negative feelings **about** negative feelings. For instance:

"Even though I hate that I'm angry at my baby daughter for crying all night, I love and accept myself."

"Even though I feel guilty about resenting my husband, I love and accept myself."

Step 2: Tap on your "karate chop" point three times with your fingers while saying your affirmation (either out loud or in your head). This acupressure point is located on the edge of your hand, about an inch down from where your pinky joins the palm (hence the name of this point). Use pressure that feels comfortable, neither too hard nor too light. I use my index and middle fingers for tapping, although it is also fine to use your intuition as far as determining how you would like to tap. Some people find that rubbing the EFT acupressure spots is also effective. It doesn't matter which of your hands (dominant or non-dominant) you use for tapping or rubbing.

When you are done with your karate chop point, take several deep breaths and then measure your distress from zero to ten again. Notice if the number has stayed the same, gone up or moved down. Depending on what the number is, you might want to modify the affirmation or keep it the same (more on that below).

Step 3: Now you will tap for about five seconds on each of the points that I will describe below. As you do so, you will use a shortened form of your affirmation. Just use the words that describe what is bothering you. So if your affirmation was "Even though I feel overwhelmed by work, I love and accept myself," then the shortened version would simply be "feeling overwhelmed." Other examples:

"This anger at my father"

"feeling stressed"

"this headache"

"anxiety about flying"

"Craving sweets"

The first point is on the crown of your head. Next, tap on your eyebrows, right above the bridge of your nose. Then move to your temples, where your eyebrows end. The next points are directly under your eyes, on the eye sockets. These three points around the eyes obviously occur on each side of your body, so my recommendation is to use your hands to tap on both sides at the same time.

Next is a point on your filtrum (that little indentation right under your nose). Then you move to a point directly under your bottom lip (known as the chin point). The last two points I'd like you to tap on are known as the collar bone points. You can locate them by first feeling for your sternal notch (where the knot of a tie would go). Bring your fingertips down about an inch from that spot, and then move them away from each other about an inch. In order to ensure that you hit these points, use four fingers instead of two for tapping. The full EFT protocol includes several more points, but the abbreviated version I have provided here is a great start that will certainly give you emotional relief.

Step 4: Congratulations! You've just completed a round of EFT. Now pay attention to how you feel. The goal is to bring your distress level to a zero. If the first round of tapping has not done that, you have two options. You could repeat the round of tapping, starting with the karate chop point, stating "Even though I **still** [have this problem], I love and accept myself." Your reminder phrase would be "still [description of problem]".

Your other option is to change the language of your initial affirmation. It could be that something else is actually causing your distress. For example, instead of focusing on your headache, it might be more fruitful to say, "Even though I am stressed about my relationship, I love and accept myself." Or, while you feel angry about getting in a fight with your son, what is also happening beneath that emotion is sadness about the situation, in which case you would state, "Even though I am sad that I got into a fight with my son, I love and accept myself."

Now that you have a good sense of what EFT entails, let me explain why I recommend using it. First, it is quick and convenient. You can do it anywhere, anytime. Second, it allows you to own your emotions by giving you an excuse to verbally express how you are truly feeling. Third, EFT gives you something physical to do with yourself when you are dealing with difficult emotions. So not only is it healing, but also a great distraction that can keep you from ruminating. Finally, EFT gives you the opportunity to remind yourself that even though you might be distressed by your emotions, you can still love and accept yourself. That is, it is OK and perfectly normal to have conflicting feelings at the same time: feeling angry at your child/loving your child/loving yourself. People often beat themselves up because they feel upset about feelings they are having. With EFT, you can acknowledge those feelings and then immediately pair them with a positive affirmation about yourself.

Even if you don't believe the affirmation "I love and accept myself" at first, just going through the motions will begin to affect how you feel about yourself.

As I mentioned above, there is a great deal of more detailed information about EFT on the internet. So if you this believe this tool will be helpful, please pursue it – it could make all the difference for you in creating the positive relationship with food and eating that you desire.

Conclusion

A jug fills drop by drop.

the Buddha

*Your difficulties are not obstacles on the path, they **are** the path.*

Ezra Bayda

Celebrate endings, for they precede new beginnings.

Jonathan Lockwood Huie

Congratulations! You have reached the end of *The Buddha Diet*. But it is also true that your journey with food and eating will never end. My goal with this book has been to provide you with the skills that will allow you to enjoy and appreciate what you experience on that path.

You now have everything you need in order to create a positive, healthy relationship with food and eating. So from this point, it is up to you to continue to use these tools in your everyday life. Experiment with what you have learned so that you can discover what works best for you. Remember that the more you practice, the easier it will be for you to access the skills. Soon you will notice that your new eating habits will come easily, without effort. Using your skills will become like second nature. As Ch'ing-yüan Wei-hsin wrote so long ago:

Before I had studied Zen for thirty years, I saw mountains as mountains, and waters as waters. When I arrived at a more intimate knowledge, I came to the point where I saw that mountains are not mountains, and waters are not waters. But now that I have got its very substance I am at rest. For it's just that I see mountains once again as mountains and waters once again as waters.

My desire is also that you understand the eating of food as the beautiful, sacred act that it deserves to be. Eating is not something to be agonized over. Rather, it is a gift you give yourself. And because you have learned to like and appreciate who you are, the only thing that will make sense is to treat yourself with kindness.

Of course, this perspective can be widely applied. For if you can approach other things in your life besides eating with that same sense of attention, consideration, compassion and deliberation, just imagine how the quality of your experiences will change!

***

The ordinary arts we practice every day at home are of more importance to the soul than their simplicity might suggest.

Thomas Moore

If you live the sacred and despise the ordinary, you are still bobbing in the ocean of delusion.

Zen Master Lin-Chi

There are only two ways to live your life. One is as though nothing is a miracle. The other is as though everything is a miracle.

Albert Einstein

Before I conclude *The Buddha Diet*, I do have one more thing to ask of you.

You may recall that in chapter 5 you created a mission statement for your life. Now I would like you to conclude this program by creating a mission statement in which you describe your ideal relationship with food and eating. Think about everything you have learned since you began reading this book. Consider your new levels of self-awareness and knowledge, and how each can help you manifest a future that is empowering for you.

As you create your mission statement, focus the place you would like food to occupy in your life. Think about the kind of connection you would like to have with what you put into your body. Also consider how you will go about preparing and eating your meals, both on a practical level as well as mentally and emotionally. This piece of writing, as the final exercise of the book, will be your master blueprint that will guide you as you move forward on your journey.

To assist you in crafting your mission statement, I offer you the following questions. Imagine how you would like to ideally answer them, and incorporate your responses into what you write.

1. How am I listening to my body?
2. Am I eating when I feel physically hungry?
3. Do I stop eating when I am satisfied?
4. How am I managing my hunger?
5. How am I managing (and honoring) my daily rhythms?
6. Am I in control of when and how I eat during the day?

7. How am I recovering if I have done something I regret?
8. How do I respond if I have made a poor food choice?
9. What am I telling myself as I consider my food choices?
10. How am I managing the portions of what I am eating?
11. How am I preventing binges?
12. How am I avoiding eating things I know I will regret?
13. How am I savoring my food?
14. How am I eating food so that it has become a sacred ritual?
15. How am I showing myself compassion?
16. How am I incorporating balance into my life?
17. How am I managing my emotions?
18. How am I focusing on being healthy?

***

From the Bhaddekaratta Sutta:

Do not pursue the past
Do not lose yourself in the future
The past no longer is
The future has not yet come
Looking deeply at life as it is
In the very here and now, the practitioner dwells in stability
and freedom
We must be diligent today
To wait until tomorrow is too late
Death comes unexpectedly
How can we bargain with it?
The sage calls a person who knows how to dwell in
mindfulness night and day,
'one who knows the better way to live alone.'

A monk told Joshu: "I have just entered the monastery. Please teach me." Joshu asked, "Have you eaten your rice porridge?" The monk replied, "I have eaten." Joshu said: "Then you had better wash your bowl." At that moment the monk was enlightened.

Zen story

About the Author

My name is Andy Matzner. I'm a psychotherapist and life coach. I have a master's degree in social work and have been licensed as a clinical social worker since 2006.

My mission is twofold. First, to empower people to experience their full potential. Second, to assist people in finding relief from frustration and pain.

I follow a holistic perspective and believe that our quality of life depends on having a sense of balance in our lives. This means paying attention not only to our mental and emotional health, but also to our bodies and spiritual sides as well.

I've been interested in alternative and complementary medicine for many years, especially energy psychology and vibrational healing. I have studied acutonics, emotional freedom techniques (EFT) and hypnosis, and have completed Reiki I and II training. In addition, I enjoy using Tibetan and crystal singing bowls with individuals and groups – the tones of these instruments produce deep states of relaxation very easily.

I also love to teach. I started in 1992 as a Latin instructor at the University of Hawaii. From there I taught English as a Second Language while living abroad in Thailand (2 years), Japan (1 year), and Australia (6 months).

Currently I live with my family in rural southwest Virginia. I have been teaching undergraduate and graduate courses at Hollins University as an adjunct professor in the Gender and Women's Studies Department for over ten years. And since 2010 I've been teaching mental health and psychology classes at Virginia Western Community College.

You can learn more about my counseling and coaching practice at http://andymatzner.com

20800744R00126

Made in the USA
Charleston, SC
28 July 2013